Selling to a Group

Selling to a Group

▶ *Presentation Strategies* ◀

Paul LeRoux

Illustrations by VanSeveren

BARNES & NOBLE BOOKS
A DIVISION OF HARPER & ROW, PUBLISHERS
New York, Cambridge, Philadelphia, San Francisco
London, Mexico City, São Paulo, Singapore, Sydney

SELLING TO A GROUP. Copyright © 1984 by Paul LeRoux. All rights reserved.
Printed in the United States of America. No part of this book may be used or
reproduced in any manner whatsoever without written permission except in the case
of brief quotations embodied in critical articles and reviews. For information address Harper & Row, Publishers, Inc., 10 East 53rd Street, New York, N.Y. 10022.
Published simultaneously in Canada by Fitzhenry & Whiteside Limited, Toronto.

FIRST EDITION

Designer: Abigail Sturges

Library of Congress Cataloging in Publication Data

LeRoux, Paul.
    Selling to a group.

    Bibliography: p.
    Includes index.
    1. Communication in management. 2. Public speaking.
3. Business report writing. I. Title.
HF5718.L46 1984   658.4′52   84-47586
ISBN 0-06-015345-8   84 85 86 87 88 10 9 8 7 6 5 4 3 2 1
ISBN 0-06-463598-8 (pbk.)   84 85 86 87 88 10 9 8 7 6 5 4 3 2 1

Contents

Preface

This book is not about public speaking—it's about selling to groups. There are similarities between a business presentation and a speech. However, selling to a group involves a different set of problems and opportunities from giving speeches.

As a communications consultant, I've helped scores of companies win competitive presentations and coached hundreds of executives to be successful presenters at large national meetings and stockholder gatherings. My company regularly creates visuals for competitive presentations. These consulting projects are done for accounting, law, actuarial, engineering, and architectural firms across the country. The presentations are usually given to an executive committee, board of directors, or a jury. The stakes can be very high.

I wrote this book because I am appalled at how much wrong, stupid, even harmful advice is given about selling to groups.

Wrong advice, such as "It's better to sit around the table and keep it informal."

Worthless advice, like "The group will love you—don't worry"; "Rise to the occasion"; or "Remember the communication process: sender, message, receiver, and feedback."

Harmful advice, like "Play with a pencil, use a pointer, or suppress the jitters by slipping your hand in your pocket, or hide nervousness by standing behind the lectern."

Crippling advice, like "The best way to organize your presentation is to write it, word for word."

And the two worst pieces of advice: "Use word/number visuals, and in front of a large group, read your message."

For convincing, persuading, selling your ideas, products, services, or point of view to a group, here's advice that pays immediately. No theory, no baloney, just good, solid techniques that have helped win hundreds of competitive presentations.

> *If a man empties his purse into his head, no one can take it away from him. An investment in knowledge always pays the best interest.*—Benjamin Franklin

Acknowledgments

I'm fortunate to have George Kell and Joe Floren as friends and business associates.

George Kell spent as much time reviewing this material as I spent writing it.

As a writing consultant and teacher, none surpass Joe Floren. From Joe I've borrowed ideas for Chapter 3, "Persuasion and Organization."

And last, my thanks to my mother and father who, by their own example, gave me the courage to start my own business.

Selling to a Group

Can you spot the 10 biggest mistakes in this presentation?

1. Wrong visuals. p. 61
2. Overhead—worst media. p. 103
3. Shouldn't use lectern. p. 117
4. Shouldn't use pointer. p. 20
5. Wrong position for the screen. p. 113
6. Wrong type of handout. p. 137
7. Wrong presentation stance. p. 18
8. Shouldn't use microphone. p. 117
9. Shouldn't use script. p. 4
10. No eye contact. p. 28

►1◄

Mistakes

All candidates run on virtually the same platform, so what they actually say is not a factor. What is important is how good they are at saying it.—Robert J. Ringer

---

►Not Taking Control

Presentations are painful. They're time-consuming and often expensive.

Selling is tough enough without the pressure and nervousness that strike most people when they face a group. We all know it's risky. Most presenters tarnish their images; few walk away heroes.

So, when it's time to sell to a group, many say, "Look, why don't we just sit around the table and let the presentation be an informal discussion?"

This rationale is always compelling. The arguments:

- There won't be any nervous presenters.
- Preparing visuals is expensive, a logistical nightmare, and will be perceived by the viewer as overkill or canned.

With those reasons, it's understandable why most opt to sell sitting down. *But the rationale is faulty.* This story tells why.

I have a good client who is the managing partner of a major international accounting firm. He's a strong believer in concise proposals and persuasive presentations.

One day he called me with an assignment to help him retain a client who had shifted headquarters from Houston to the Midwest. The client felt the move was a good time to solicit other accounting-firm proposals. Five presentations were lined up.

The day before the presentation, we had a rehearsal. As the communications consultant, I started the meeting by asking the team to stand and run through their parts. Rehearsals are never easy, especially when you're being critiqued in front of your peers by an outsider.

Right after I announced my plan, a Houston partner launched his reasons why we didn't need to stand up and go through all that jazz. Besides, he had known the client personally for many years. Why couldn't the team just sit around the table and have an informal discussion?

I knew my client, the managing partner, was calling the shots and, in the end, we'd go my way. I also knew he expected me to sell my ideas nice and easy. So we spent the next hour discussing delivery techniques, visuals—the works. Finally, the managing partner said, "Why don't we get up and try it? Let's see what happens."

I had known the Houston partner for only about an hour and sized him up as a nice guy but with a lot of excuses to cover his uncertainties about the upcoming performance. He would be, I thought, about average—no better or worse than hundreds of others I had seen stumble through rehearsals.

Surprise! After the first minute of his presentation I knew he was one of those rare people who are fantastic on their feet. Yes, he had a few glitches and was irritated when I suggested corrections, but it didn't matter. He was an outstanding presenter.

Here is my point: I, the communications expert, sat across the conference table from this guy and rated him as average. Seconds after he got on his feet, I realized my mistake—we had an excellent presenter on the team.

What happened? Simple. When you're a good presenter, you'll have ten times the "command presence" standing that you'll ever have seated.

I suspect you're thinking, "Yeah, but when you're not so hot standing, like most people, the negatives can far outweigh the positives!" True. But let's stick with one point at a time. *If* you could be as good standing as seated (and that's what Chapter 2 covers) you'd come across much more convincingly.

Would a coach whose team is losing grab a chair and sit down to deliver his half-time message? If you knew, as you walked into your boss's office, that you were going to be fired immediately, would you prefer to stand or sit? People even say, "He or she won't take that sitting down!" Haven't you often stood, paced, and gestured during an important phone conversation?

When we really want to make a point, we do it best standing. We're more dominating, especially if the others stay seated. We appear more forceful because we use larger gestures and speak more loudly. When you stand, you and your message are the center of attention.

Think of it in terms of persuasion. Even if you're selling to just one or two people around a conference table, consider standing.

My client won the presentation shootout. The other competing firms sat around the table and had nice little discussions. To the listeners, they didn't stand out. Accountants dress alike, talk alike, have similar fees, and all appear to be nice folks. There are differences, of course, but they're subtle and hard to spot. Stand, present well, and you'll make subtle differences into big differences.

▶Reading a Presentation

What I have to say is, I believe, far too important to write down on paper. I prefer to write on my audience's mind, on their emotions, with every ounce of my being. A piece of paper cannot stand between me and those I want to impress.
—Charles F. Kettering, director of General Motors

If you've forgotten how bad reading a presentation is, I'll recreate the scene for you. The chairman carries a stack of pages to the lectern. After laying them down, he grips the sides of the lectern, hunches forward, and starts reading. He reads a couple of lines, then quickly glances at the listeners. This continues for a few pages until he loses his place or feels an eyestrain headache coming on.

Quickly he concludes, "The hell with glancing at the group. If I do that anymore, I'll stumble again." So the chairman stops glancing at the group and just reads away. Presenters delude themselves into thinking that, because they're now comfortable, it's coming across better.

At first the presenter has our attention, especially if he or she is the executive vice president, boss, senior partner, or senator. These folks walk on water, don't they? We don't see them often, so it's a chance to observe Zeus. After a few minutes, however, looking at the speaker gets old. Our attention begins to wander for two reasons: nothing is happening, and reading aloud in itself is boring.

1. *Nothing is happening.*   Since the presenter is gripping the lectern, he rarely gestures. Even if we're listening, we find ourselves looking at the next person's clothing, the floor, and our watches. Our eyes wander because there is no action (movement) at the lectern. In searching for something more interesting, we still hear the words. Or so we think. Unfortunately, our subconscious subtly turns off the noise (words). We do this very

effectively in our offices or elevators to block out that schmaltzy piped-in music. As our attention wanes, we fill the void by daydreaming or thinking about other things. We'll miss most of what's said at the lectern. It happens every Sunday morning to millions of churchgoers.

2. *Reading is boring.*   You want to be labeled a dull person? Read a presentation. Here is a typical example. It involved the president of a large bank. When he learned he was to be the key speaker at a national bankers' meeting, he called his PR director and told him to start drafting a presentation. The PR director sweated many hours over the project.

The bank president sat at a speakers' table in a ballroom filled with about four hundred other bankers. Just before he was to speak, the PR director crept up and whispered, "Here's the last-minute version with the corrections you wanted." Shortly after, the president took the script, walked up to the lectern, laid the ten pages down and started reading his message to the audience.

He read the first eight pages with no problems. Then disaster struck. There had been a slight collating accident—a duplicate of page 8. He read page 8 all over again. He didn't realize what he had done. But it didn't matter. Few in the audience realized his mistake either! Everyone had long since tuned out.

Think about the entertainment value of reading presentations. How many folks would *pay* to hear presidents *read* their annual stockholders' message? Try making money selling television rights to commencement addresses. All these dull presentations have one thing in common—the presenters *read* their messages while hiding behind a lectern.

Reading a presentation is boring because:

• There is little eye contact.
• There are few gestures.

- Presenters hide two-thirds of their bodies behind the lectern.
- The presenter's voice settles into a monotone.

You don't rise in business if you're a dullard. In fact, those who survive the corporate gauntlet are usually forceful, enthusiastic, quick-witted people. But let an executive read a presentation, and what do you have? An individual who suddenly seems to be a different person. Reading a presentation blocks all the individuality of the presenter.

Yet so many presenters grip the lectern and read away. Why? Some presenters procrastinate, so at the last minute they scribble out their ideas, and have to read them. Most simply believe reading is the *only* way. "Sure," they reply, "if I had nothing else to do for two weeks, I could memorize this darned thing and it would sound terrific, but I just don't have two weeks to do that."

Well, there is another way, and the good news is that it will save you time, and you will come across as the dynamic person you are.

First question: Why write a script at all? You certainly won't write a script for a one-to-one conversation. Why do it for a presentation?

Why Read a Presentation?

Let's say you're an accountant, and you're in a plane seated next to the financial officer of a large corporation. After exchanging amenities, he asks, "How do I know if I'm getting the best service from my accounting firm?"

Would you reach into your briefcase, pull out a pad of paper, and say, "I'll write down a few ideas, organize them, practice a few times, and right after lunch we'll talk"?

Of course, you wouldn't. You would give him a terrific off-the-cuff answer. Your reply could last ten to forty minutes.

After you parted, you might even congratulate yourself on what a nifty conversation you stimulated.

Imagine yourself as that same accounting partner in another scene. You've just been invited to be the key speaker at the National Association of Finance Officers' yearly gathering. Your topic is "How to Evaluate Accounting Services."

Isn't this how that scene would unfold? Two weeks before the presentation you would pull out the pad of paper, and you would write out a full script, and at the meeting you would read most of your presentation. Afterward, you'd feel a bit shabby because it didn't go as well as you'd have liked. You'd rationalize that, if you hadn't been so busy and if you'd had more time to practice, you would have been your usual dynamic self.

Let's look at the difference. On the plane you had no script, no time to practice, and you spoke very well. However, you had to face only one person, and you had a ninety-minute plane ride to make your point. As the key speaker you had a script, had run through it a few times, and performed less than spectacularly. But you had to face many people, and you had only twenty minutes to make your point.

Since you did so well off the cuff, why not be more conversational in front of a group? At stake is impressing three hundred prospects. Your goal is to come across as ten times more knowledgeable, dynamic, and creative than those who are currently their accountants.

Of course, you're nervous in front of a group—and more likely to forget something. But reading a script and being dull won't overcome the problem. Nervousness does make it harder to keep the content rolling, but nervousness doesn't mean you'll draw a complete blank. (Remember, on the plane you needed no script and no practice.)

▶The Alternative to Reading

Under the pressure of a large audience I wouldn't expect you to remember the sequence of all your major points and their subpoints. But you could remember your ideas if you were cued.

Therefore, write on a five-by-eight card (three-by-five is too small) only a couple of words describing your main point and underneath a couple of words for three or four subpoints. *For these cards use key words or phrases, not complete sentences.*

When the time comes to speak, pause, look down at the card, jog your memory, and deliver your first point. After you've said all you can remember about that point and its subpoints, go back to the lectern; pause, look down at the card to see if you've covered everything. If you forgot something worth mentioning, look back at the group and continue. When you've finished, pause, turn the card over and put it aside, jog

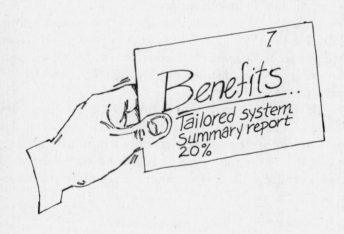

Lectern Cue Card

your memory from the next card, move to the side of the lectern, and continue again. (Write on only *one side* of each card and number all your cards.)

As you become more comfortable with the audience, you'll hardly need the cards. That shouldn't surprise you. On the plane you had no cues. The cards are a crutch—your insurance. The cards are memory joggers. They provide a way to appear extemporaneous with a safety net. The cards are not a script. Don't be tempted to fill them with sentences or you'll end up with a sixty-card script and be back in Dullsville.

Trust yourself. You won't forget what you have to say. You've had much more time to organize your ideas than you had on the plane. Your message will be more compact and logical. Therefore, it will have more punch and persuasion if you don't read it.

Step up to the lectern, lay your cards on the ledge, then take a step to the side. That step assures that you won't grip the sides or lean on the lectern. If you're gripping the sides, you won't be gesturing. Look to the back of the room, lock in with eye contact on the furthermost person, pause for three seconds, and start.

The lectern is a barrier between the audience and the presenter. It hides 70 percent of a presenter's body. The microphone distorts the voice. Turn down the lights for slides, and even the presenter's facial expressions are lost. Too many large-group presentations become voices in the dark. The delivery couldn't be more impersonal, dull, and ineffective.

Stepping to the side, away from the lectern, suddenly places you on much more personal terms with the audience. The barrier is gone. Your move tells the group that you wish to be closer to them and that what you have to say is personal and created just for them. *The secret to a successful presentation is to get away from both reading and hiding behind the lectern.*

Presenting from the side of the lectern allows you to be seen, to be more natural, to be in a better position to burn off nervous energy, and, most important, to appear more believable and convincing.

Reading tells the audience that the presentation isn't very important—or that you didn't have enough time to do anything better. Since you're good in conversation, there is no reason to read a presentation. You're best when you're natural. Why give the audience anything less?

Reading Leads to Disaster

Very few chief executives are good on their feet. Whoever writes the speeches, the CEO delivers them atrociously.—David Ogilvy

Here are two disasters from many. I hope they cure your itch to read a presentation.

A few years ago, I helped an executive vice president of a large oil company train his senior executives for a company-sponsored speakers' bureau. We celebrated the end of this training with a big dinner party. The afternoon before the dinner, the company president had an important analysts' meeting. He felt he didn't need any training to be part of his company's speakers' bureau, so I went to the analysts' meeting to see how good he really was. It was the week before Christmas.

The president launched into reading a fifteen-minute report of financial earnings and the latest company accomplishments. As he plowed through, I thought, "What a shame; if only he had ventured into a few of our sessions, he wouldn't be boring everyone." He ended his remarks by reading: ". . . and I would like to wish you all Merry [pause while he turned the page] Christmas and a happy New Year." How insincere can you get!

Surely he was capable of wishing everyone season's greetings without notes! Reading a presentation will trip you every time. You're not thinking; you're simply mouthing a script.

There is one college inauguration I will never forget. It was

"*Ooh-aiy-eee-argh-ow-yow-ooo...*"

typical of other inaugurations I had attended, with one exception. After the seal was officially passed from the old president to the new, the old president moved toward the lectern. The new president started to return to his chair to sit down. (Normally it's the other way around, because the new president will remain standing to start his inaugural address. In this case, the former president had said earlier that he wanted to say a few words.)

As the new president started for his chair, the former president said, "No, please come and stand next to me where I can look at you, because what I have to say is really to you." With that opening line, you could suddenly hear yourself breathe. He had everyone's attention. What I experienced for the next ten minutes was one of the most moving speeches I have ever heard. The former president told the new president he must not let the administrative duties overwhelm him; he must listen to the students and the faculty, and set aside time to think about his place in the world and his responsibilities.

The message was important, but much more than the words moved the audience. They sensed and were touched by the deep love this president had for his college.

Everything about that speech was perfect. The message was appropriate, the presenter had excellent eye contact and a loud, strong voice, and his skill in using pauses was the best I've ever heard. He paced his words so that each idea had time to be tasted and weighed; but, most important, he had emotion and spoke without notes. To have stood three feet apart and read the message would have been to rip the heart from his delivery.

The old president finished with an ending that was as powerful as his opening lines. There was silence—we were overwhelmed by his feelings and sincerity. Then there were a cheering and clapping that matched the emotions he had stirred.

I was attending the inauguration because the new president had his doctorate in rhetoric and public address and had previously chaired the speech department at the college he left. I would see, I thought, a pro's performance.

As the old president sat down, I was thinking, "What a tough act to follow; if ever a presenter could be rattled by the success of the previous speaker, this would be the time." That is probably what happened. I had already heard the new president speak off the cuff at a large luncheon gathering, and he was very good. But, for his inaugural address, he unfortunately read his message. Too bad. His ideas may have been as brilliant as his predecessor's, but they never left the page.

Reading a presentation will always choke sincerity, conviction, and credibility. When I work with clients who lean toward reading, I begin by videotaping ten minutes of their presentation. Then I find an associate who speaks only from brief notes and put that performance on video. The playbacks and a little coaching are all it takes to convince "readers" to change their ways.

Now the problem is how to perform well on your feet without the security of a script and without a lectern. Over lunch we're dynamite, but most of us are not comfortable when we have to stand at the end of the board-room table or at a lectern. Few people sell as well one-to-group as they do one-to-one. The next chapter tells you the delivery skills you'll need to stand and sell your ideas.

►2◄

Delivery Skills and Presentation Know-How

Your words are not the message—you are.

►Handling Nervousness

Nervous energy gnaws at most presenters. So the first thing we do is try to hold back what's developing in our bodies. We can feel a herd of elephants rendezvousing in our stomachs. To head off their charge, we do strange things.

Behind a lectern, we grip the sides so hard our knuckles turn white. If we've been in the military and have no lectern, we immediately clasp our hands behind us at "parade rest." Without a lectern, we have only ourselves to hang on to. Our hands become like magnets—either clasped behind the back in "parade rest" or in front in the "fig-leaf" position.

A popular posture for men is one hand jammed in the pants pocket with the elbow of the other arm held tightly against the side, restricting the hand to small, slow circles in front of the chest.

Women achieve the same effect by locking one forearm across the midriff, holding the other elbow. The free hand keeps time with the cadence of the voice.

What kinds of gestures result from these postures? Small gestures, ineffectual gestures, funny gestures. With the hands

Nervous Presenters

Wrong Presentation Stances

locked onto some part of the body, nothing much can happen. When the moment comes to emphasize the words, the body tries to respond. But it can't, because it's locked. The most it can manage is a flick of the fingers or the wrist.

No wonder people tell me they're exhausted at the end of a twenty-minute presentation. With a locked posture, presenting becomes an isometric exercise. Something in us is trying to gesture, but some other part of us is trying to stifle any movement.

Why do we tie ourselves up like that? I don't think it's unintentional; we do it on purpose. We're afraid that, if we let ourselves go, we'll make some wild, indiscreet, or inappropriate gesture. We're afraid that our bodies are going to betray us. But that almost never happens. Our bodies want to *help* us—if we'll let them.

Your nervous system reacts to a presentation by releasing adrenalin into your bloodstream. The purpose of the adrenalin is to give your body a boost so that it can meet what appears to be a threat or challenge. The adrenalin prepares the body, psychologists say, for "fight or flight."

One way or another, nervous energy will surface. Like a volcano, nervousness starts from below—in the feet. That's why so many presenters pace back and forth. You can't stop nervousness. It's a reaction to the adrenalin. But you can harness nervousness. The problem is that most presenters don't know how. So the energy leaks out negatively. Trying to suppress nervous energy is like crimping a water hose. You reduce the water flow, but the pressure causes the hose to squirm and wiggle.

The trick in handling nervous energy is to burn it off positively instead of having it flare uncontrolled. This is done in three ways: by a correct stance, supporting gestures, and a loud voice.

The Stance

If you're going to have your body help you make the presentation, you must start from a posture that will let it do its work.

Face the group, feet ten to twelve inches apart. Keep your weight equally distributed. Don't shift your weight from one leg to the other. Your knees should be unlocked, your hands out of your pockets, your arms at your sides.

The stance described above is for both sexes. Women have a tendency in presentations to lift the toe of one shoe and rock their foot about on the heel. It's distracting.

Start every presentation in this neutral position. But you won't stay neutral long. Once you unlock your hands and arms and are standing in the neutral position, you'll find you're using gestures to support your message. You'll be shifting your weight. Strong, authoritative gestures use both the arms and body.

It's okay to move as long as your movements and gestures support or add to your message. You may take a step or two, but don't pace back and forth. That's negative use of nervous energy. Pacing doesn't support your message. It's just nervousness surfacing negatively, and it's a distraction. Between gestures, return to the neutral position.

The neutral position will feel unnatural at first. It should. For years, you've stood at a parade-rest, fig-leaf, or hands-in-pockets position. Any long-standing habit is hard to break.

Gestures

> *Action seems to follow feeling, but really action and feeling go together; and by regulating the action, which is under the more direct control of the will, we can indirectly regulate the feeling, which is not.*—William James

An excellent way to channel nervous energy is through gestures. When we are *not* under the pressure of a presentation, we use gestures freely and effectively. We always give directions with gestures. It is so natural to point or bend your palm as you say, "Then take a left. . . ."

Some people are much more energetic than others. Consequently, they gesture more. Many people are unable to say a single sentence without moving their hands. Others gesture less, but most of us use a lot of gestures in conversation.

Gestures serve three purposes in a presentation:

- to release nervous energy
- to hold listener attention
- to support one's message visually

I'm sure you'll agree that burning off nervous energy with gestures looks better than standing there fingering the coins in your pocket or turning your ring.

The eye is drawn to three things: color, noise, and movement—the color of your clothes, the noise of your voice, and any movement of your body.

What's fascinating about watching logs burn in a fireplace? All three elements are there: the multicolors, the crackling noise, and the leaping flames.

Movement (gesturing) is a critical element of every presentation if you want to hold the listener's attention.

To hold attention and support your message, you must have large gestures. Unfortunately, using gestures is a problem for many executives. When they were children, they were great with gestures, as children usually are. As they grew older, however, they became more self-conscious and inhibited about using their bodies in formal settings like presentations. To be reserved, conservative, and quiet is a trademark of the pin-striped-suit crowd. That's okay in the executive suite, but it makes for a stiff and dull presenter.

I'm not asking you to become the circus barker. I'm simply recommending that you use your body to support what you are saying. Every verb is an excellent source for a supportive gesture.

Slash expenses before . . .
Regulations *are choking* us.
We'll pull you through this problem.

Descriptive terms or phrases are other good sources for gestures. For example,

There is a *huge mix-up* in the warehouse.
Profits have headed *south.*
The sky's the limit for this promotion.

Be articulate with the gestures, or they will deteriorate into cocktail-party hand waving. Cocktail gestures are usually hands in front of the chest, moving in little circles. With cocktail gestures you burn off little nervous energy and are doing nothing to support your message. Cocktail gestures do not hold the listeners' attention for long, *because every gesture is the same.*

With your hands out of your pockets, you will now use your hands and arms much more freely. But be careful. If you don't return to the neutral position between gestures, you'll find your hands continually coming together like those of a praying mantis!

Negative Gestures

In addition to clasped hands and cocktail gestures, there are other undesirable hand movements. Nervous energy leaks out negatively when presenters touch their bodies. They pull at their ears, rub their cheeks, push at the bridge of their glasses, or tug at their coat-pocket flaps.

Don't touch your body—period. The moment your hands move to touch some part of your body, the listeners' eyes are pulled to that movement. So leave your body alone. As your hand moves to caress yourself, your conscience should remind you, "Hey, don't touch."

During a presentation you should not hold pointers, pen-

Gestures

cils, pens, pieces of paper, microphones, or the projector's remote-control switch. Things in your hand suddenly acquire lives of their own.

Folks with collapsible pointers will absentmindedly pull out the extensions, then push them back in. The more nervous they are, the more they'll play with the pointers. Presenters with wooden pointers will pretend they're in the military and slap their legs with their swagger sticks, or play orchestra leader as they wave their new batons about.

If you're holding a pencil, you'll continually roll or twirl it. Of course, you'll drop the darned thing during your presentation and everyone will have to watch you stoop to retrieve it.

The best pointers are your arms and hands. Learn to underscore with your hand. Don't point with your finger: It can look weak or, worse, vaguely obscene. And don't make the mistake of covering what you're pointing to. Underscoring is like a karate chop—a strong, authoritative gesture. With underscoring you'll burn nervous energy positively, and be *part* of the message rather than a distraction.

If you're carrying a marker, you'll be pulling the cap on and off. The listeners' eyes will be focused on the movement— your hands, the cap, and how well you can talk and recap at the same time. You won't always recap it perfectly. You'll jab the point into a finger—a distraction that pulls attention away from your words.

Playing with things in your hands is bad enough. But a bigger damage is that the *nervous energy goes into the hand playing instead of into gestures that support your message.*

Voice Volume

One of the side effects of adrenalin pumping through the body is that you'll get a dry mouth and a tense throat. To overcome this, many speakers drink cold water just before they present. This helps the dry mouth, but it's a mistake for the tense throat

Pointers: Swagger Sticks . . .

. . . and Orchestra Leaders

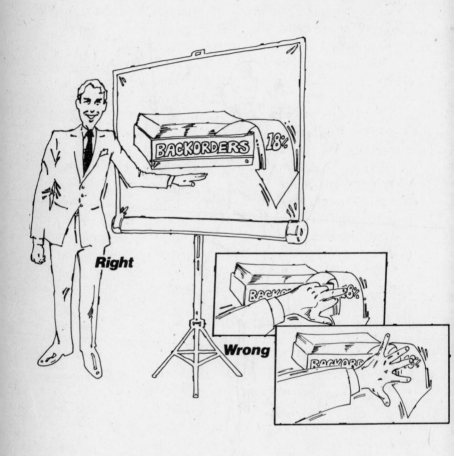

Underscoring

muscles. Cold things *tighten* muscles. The best drink, therefore, is something hot, such as tea, coffee, or cocoa.

If there is nothing available to drink, lightly chew your tongue. Go ahead! Try it now . . . in fifteen seconds, you'll have all the saliva you need to overcome a dry mouth.

When presenters start, they are very nervous. Their voices are low. Suddenly, they cough, put their hands to their mouths, and say, "Excuse me." You've seen it many times. You know it's not a cough, but rather that the presenter's voice died because he or she was very nervous and choked. This is nervous energy using the presenter.

The way to overcome this is to speak *loudly.* This is especially important when you start. A presenter's voice is like a car on a cold winter morning. If you don't give your car enough gas, it sputters and dies. Your voice will do the same when you're nervous. *You must begin with high volume.*

To gain higher volume, direct your presentation to someone sitting in the back of the room. The tendency is to start a presentation by looking at the person closest to you. When you speak to the closest person, your volume naturally will be lower than if you project it to the back of the room. Start with high volume and *direct at least your first ten seconds to one person in the back.*

Since a woman's voice doesn't always project as well as a man's, she needs to make an extra effort to start with ample volume, or her voice will choke and fade more often than a man's. No, a microphone is not the answer. See "The Microphone . . ." on page 117.

Even though you probably have a softer voice than your male co-worker, there is no reason to come across as timid or less forceful. More volume will help control your stress. WOMEN, SPEAK UP.

I often have trouble persuading executives to speak loudly enough. Their rebuttal is "It sounds too loud. It feels like I'm shouting." The presenter's voice always sounds louder to the presenter than it does to the listeners. Presenters hear their own voices with more than just their ears. They "hear" the sound as it vibrates through the bone structure of the skull.

A louder voice commands attention. When you raise your volume, you'll gesture, nod, and smile more; you'll be more animated; you'll ooze enthusiasm and conviction. Just the traits you need when you're trying to sell your ideas in front of a group. All this happens when you raise your voice. I certainly don't mean shouting, but I do mean a healthy, strong projection.

The merit of higher volume is what it does for nervous energy. Higher volume burns off energy. Nervous energy must go somewhere. When you channel nervous energy into higher volume, you are using it positively.

▶ Eye Contact—The Silent Persuader

To make oneself understood to people, one must first speak to their eyes.—Napoleon

Presenters pay little attention to eye contact because they think they already know all about it. The truth is that very, very few presenters know how to look at listeners. Yet eye contact is one of the most important persuaders you can use in selling to a group.

We've developed a terrible habit. It began in grade school when the teacher told us to stand and give our first book report in front of the class. The teacher probably said, "Look up, and speak to the whole class." It didn't take us long to learn how to look at the class and quickly take in every face in the room. This bad habit even has a name. It's called "scanning."

As we progressed from grade-school book reports to college debates to business presentations, scanning became a deeply embedded habit. Scanning gains acceptance on the premise that moving the eye about the room keeps listeners involved. The assumption is false. Looking at people to involve them is certainly important, but moving the eyes *quickly* through the group is harmful.

Why Scanning Causes Problems

The mind is a fantastic computer. It can process information in fractions of a second. As a presenter scans the listeners, every image, every movement, every color the eye sees must be processed. The brain does this very fast, but each bit still must be processed. The brain thinks about each bit, rejects it, stores it, or reacts to it. *The faster the eyes scan, the more visual information the brain must process.*

However, that isn't the only information the brain is processing. At the same time the eyes are bringing in visual information, the brain is working feverishly to develop ideas and deliver words. These two processing systems can collide. When that happens, both activities come to a halt.

I'm sure you can recall seeing a presenter with this problem. Two things happen. First, talking becomes confused and slows to a stop. Then the eyes look to the ceiling or the floor (or they actually close). These reactions allow time to untangle the processing machinery before restarting it.

Notice how nervous energy and eye contact work together. The faster the presenter scans, the more nervous he or she appears. Having to process visual information rapidly seems to put the whole body on a faster and faster treadmill. The faster the eyes move, the more visual information the presenter has to process. The brain seems to react by telling other body functions to speed up. The voice goes into high gear. Shifting, fidgeting, and hand wringing increase.

We've all seen the management trainee who had to get up in front of the whole department to give a short presentation. His eyes darted rapidly, his voice raced, and he madly fingered the change in his pocket. He looked uncomfortable; consequently, he appeared insincere or not in control of the situation.

Rapidly changing eye contact is always a sign of a presenter headed for trouble.

How to Correct Scanning

The way to slow down this treadmill and prevent the processing systems from colliding is to reduce the rate of incoming images. In other words, hold your focus on each listener separately instead of sweeping the eye through the group.

Longer eye contact diminishes the number of visual images that the brain must deal with in a given time. Extended eye contact allows the brain to concentrate on processing your message.

I define "scanning" as focusing a half second or less before moving. Effective eye contact focuses on each listener for *three full seconds or longer.*

At first, three-second eye contact will seem as if you're staring at someone. Looking at one person in the audience for that long will feel unnatural. That's because for years you've been scanning. It's become a habit and will be very hard to break. But the effort is well worth it, because scanning in a presentation causes many problems besides making you less persuasive.

Benefits of Extended Eye Contact

Extended eye contact will moderate your speech. It restrains shifting feet and meaningless gestures. When you use extended eye contact, your gestures will become more significant and supportive of your message.

If you think extended eye contact in a presentation appears unnatural, think about eye contact in one-to-one conversation. Aren't you offended or suspicious if someone glances about the room or looks skyward as he or she talks to you?

Next time you're in a romantic setting, notice how much eye contact is being used. People in love use eye contact extremely well. Words like "I love you," lose their credibility if your eyes are wandering around the room while you're pouring out your heart.

The difference in appearance between a scanner and a presenter who uses extended eye contact is dramatic. Presenters using three- to five-second eye contact appear more sincere, convincing, and sure of their material than the "shifty scanner."

In a presentation, extended eye contact is one of the most powerful persuaders you possess. Unless your ideas are as brilliant and concise as the parables in the book of Matthew or the Gettysburg Address, your listeners will not be hanging on every word. An excellent way to keep their attention is to look eye to eye at each person for *at least three seconds.*

When would you want to go longer than three seconds? To answer this, remember the purpose of eye contact: to stop scanning, which bombards the brain with too many images. Scanning is especially likely to happen when you are nervous. For example: you are in the middle of your presentation, everything is going well, you're moving the eye contact slowly around the room; suddenly the executive vice president bursts in, sits down, scowls at you, and glances at his watch. Immediately, your body reacts by secreting adrenalin into your bloodstream. Left unchecked, your voice will speed up, and you'll start fidgeting. Your body, of course, is pushing for ways to burn the adrenalin.

Back to the question "When should you use more than three seconds of eye contact?" The answer is, when you become very nervous. That's why it is so important in the first minute of a presentation to use extended eye contact. When you stumble, get a bad reaction from the group, or see a face reacting negatively to what you are saying, it's critical that you say to yourself, "I've got to settle down by using extended eye contact." Or, if you realize in the middle of your presentation that you've slipped back to one second per person, you must get back

"*Could we have a little eye contact?*"

on track by choosing one face and holding it for at *least three seconds* of eye contact.

Large Groups—Where to Look

In a hotel ballroom with five hundred listeners, you obviously cannot look at every face for three seconds. But, if you use extended eye contact on selected people, widely spaced, most of the five hundred will believe you've looked at them. Because of the distance between you and the listeners, when you look at one person in the crowd, ten people around that person will also get the impression that you're looking *directly* at them. Don't forget eye contact with those sitting to your extreme left and right. It is easy to neglect those in the wings.

As you master extended eye contact, you'll realize your range will vary considerably. *A good average should be about three seconds per listener.* (Scanning averages less than one second per listener.) You'll start your presentation with one person for three to ten seconds, go one second each on the next three listeners, then slow down with two five-second contacts, and so on.

As you progress to a three-second average, you'll find it helpful to finish a sentence before moving the eye contact to the next listener. Make the eye-contact duration meaningful—a sentence or a complete idea.

Learning the Technique

Very little improvement will happen if you just read about eye contact. Like tennis, golf, swimming, or other skills, it takes a lot of practice. Here are some suggestions for your practice sessions.

One-to-One

There is no better time to start improving eye contact than during one-to-one conversations. We're not bad one-to-one, but we do get careless. People say five sentences to someone, then look away during the next three sentences.

Using eye contact is like using correct verb tenses. There is no excuse for being sloppy.

Empty-Room Technique

If you rehearse a presentation in a conference room, you can practice eye contact. The larger the room, the better. Stick a piece of paper to the back of every third chair. You'll need twelve to eighteen labeled chairs and eight to twelve unlabeled ones. The idea is to look around the room, focusing on each labeled chair for three to ten seconds. As you do this, you will probably focus on each chair for only one to two seconds, because it is so easy to underestimate just how long three seconds is. To compensate for this, I would advise you to go overboard and shoot for ten seconds per labeled chair.

Hands-Up Technique

During your next presentation to friendly associates, ask everyone in the room to help you by raising one arm—as though they are signaling to ask a question. Explain to them that, when your eyes focus on one of them individually, that person is to count silently for five seconds (one thousand one, one thousand two, etc.). When he or she reaches five, the arm is lowered.

Look out at all the raised hands, pick out a face in the back, pause for three seconds, and start your delivery. Remember, you are supposed to be looking at only one person. Fight the urge to look at that person for only one second and move on.

This is the reason for the raised hands. When the listener sees you looking at him or her, he or she will start the silent five-second count. Your instructions to the group should include, "If, while you're counting, I move my eyes away to another person, give me a big smile and wave your hand."

Be sure you are eye to eye—not head, chin, nose contact but eye-to-eye contact. Once the hand goes down, you may move to the next face. Pick any face. There is no magic to the order in which you move your eyes around a room.

This is a very difficult exercise. You'll quickly see that knocking all the hands down is not easy. You'll continually want to pull away before your five seconds are finished. If you have confidence in yourself, are your own best critic, and are always seeking to improve, you'll benefit immensely from this exercise.

I'll end this section by saying again: *Extended eye contact is one of the most important "persuaders" you can use in selling to a group.*

▶ Pauses for Impact

Well-timed silence hath more eloquence than speech.
—M. T. Tupper

Pauses are powerful. Yet few presenters use them. A pause (silence) after a key point is an excellent way to emphasize and sell your message.

Think back to when you've heard presenters use a long pause before they begin. Isn't it true that the longer the pause the more you thought, "Whatever that person is going to say will be powerful."

The first place to use a pause is at the start of your presentation. Too many presenters rise from their chairs, walk to the head of the conference table, and start talking as they are turning to face the group.

Use a pause at the start to gain maximum listener attention. Walk to the front, turn slowly, select one person in the back of the room, lock in with eye contact, pause for three seconds, and then and only then start talking. If you start talking without a pause, chances are you'll begin scanning. If you pause, part of getting your act together in those silent seconds will be to lock in with eye contact.

As important as pauses are, many executives still have trouble using them. It is hard to pause when the body's adrenalin is working against you by trying to speed up your voice. But it is more than just nervousness that keeps people from reaping the benefits of pausing. People often tell me, "Yes, I see pauses work, but they just don't feel natural."

We seem to be afraid of silence. Maybe we don't like pauses because we fear the group will think we are finished or have forgotten something. Or maybe it's more deeply rooted.

We have a habit of filling in our pauses with a deplorable substitute: the words "you know." We seem to stuff "you know" in every other sentence. Where brief pauses belong, we're throwing in "you know, you know, you know." Terrible! Filler sounds like "er, uh, ah, um," have always been with us. But "you know" seems to have more recently swept the country. Like all careless filler words, it's distracting and dilutes our messages.

During a presentation, listeners need thinking space between ideas. *The more important the idea, the more important it is for the presenter to pause and let the words sink in before going to the next idea.* Pauses are necessary in presentations, just as white space is often the essential ingredient of a well-designed ad. Not having enough pauses in a presentation causes listeners to run ideas together and makes it difficult for them to distinguish major ideas from minor ones.

For example, "Gentlemen, in summary, there are three reasons to consider choosing our firm (pause, one thousand one, one thousand two). The first reason is (pause, one thousand one,

one thousand two) . . . ; the second reason is (pause, one thousand one, one thousand two) . . . ; and the third reason is (pause, one thousand one, one thousand two). . . . Thank you."

Take your time; not half-second pauses—go for two full seconds. With pauses, you'll have longer eye contact, a slower rate of speech, and more "articulate" gestures.

▶What to Wear

The clothes you wear to a presentation are important. John Molloy's books on dressing for both men and women are must reading on this topic. A white shirt or blouse still represents an honest, hard-working, sincere image. A dark suit, with a vest for men, is still the strongest symbol of power. Maybe you need to tone down your image with gray or blue and forget the tie that looks like drapery fabric or the scarf with dizzying stripes. Read Molloy's books and find out the best attire for a presentation.

Men make plenty of mistakes in their choices of clothes for presentations, but they always have one thing going for them— a jacket, a uniform. Wall Street is an avenue of clones. The sameness of it all—pin stripes, white shirts, and ties—causes me to rebel as often as possible. But when I go to clients on Wall Street, I dress like Wall Street. To do otherwise would be stupid.

Some women don't seem to like the idea of a business uniform. They tell me they get bored with wearing the same type of outfit every day. Well, I sympathize with you. All I can say is that a uniform is part of business, and without it you're swimming against a very strong current. My expertise is in presentations, not clothes. But I will tell you that a woman's clothing is more important than a man's in a presentation. A woman's outfit can seriously detract from her success. The problem is biology. If your clothes stress *la différence,* your message is being diluted.

Stress, adrenalin, and nervousness can cause one's nipples to become hard and protrude—if for that reason only, a jacket is a best bet for any presentation. It eliminates this problem and, for women, diminishes the bustline. Remember not to defeat the purpose by pushing your jacket back and standing with your hands on your hips.

▶Handling a Disaster

The worst presentation disasters always seem to involve zippers. I know the following story is true, because I was there.

The trust department of a bank was making its annual presentation to a large, important client. The bankers were to describe how well they had been managing the client's pension assets. John, the money manager who must still be vividly remembered by the client, rose to explain why the value of the bonds had nosedived.

Yes, his zipper was completely down. But the worst of it was that, every time he stuck his hands in his pockets, which was often, the opening in his trousers widened. As his hands slowly descended, I swear I could hear everyone screaming silently, "Oh God, no, John; don't put your hands in your pockets."

What should have been only an embarrassing situation suddenly turned into a disaster because John made a million excuses and thrashed about when he happened to glance down and saw the whites of his boxer shorts against his tailored pin-striped suit.

Disasters happen. Zippers go down. Blouses come unbuttoned. Pitchers tip, and water blurs your five-by-eight cards. You have just been introduced in a hotel ballroom to start your presentation, when screws in the ceiling rip loose, and the screen crashes to the floor. Or you lay your five-by-eight cards on the lectern and realize that you left half of them at the restaurant where you had breakfast.

The important point to remember about disasters is that they are *catastrophes only to the degree that you react to them.*

When the worst happens, and *if* you come unglued—it *is* a disaster! When the worst happens, pause, *quietly* panic, then accept it, because usually you must continue. Let it be only a moment's embarrassment, not a public hanging.

P.S. If, during a presentation, you find your zipper down or your blouse unbuttoned, for God's sake, do what you do when you're alone—zip it or button it. Don't make excuses, blame it on your tailor, cry, or reach for your raincoat—fix it and go on.

▶Summary

Channeling nervous energy into supportive gestures, using extended eye contact, and pausing are tough skills to master. At first, your content may suffer because your effort is being consumed by mastering delivery skills. Learning new skills and breaking old habits are difficult challenges.

Delivery skills are very physical—holding the eyes on one person, stopping the vocal cords to pause. As you master the techniques, you'll think less and less about gestures, extended eye contact, and pauses. You'll just do them, like a well-executed backhand in tennis.

Remember learning to ride a bike? The amazing part was how simple it seemed a month later. We rode without even thinking about what to do or not to do. It was as easy as breathing. Presentation skills won't stick quite that well, but they do have an immediate payoff. Use them and you'll sell your ideas more convincingly in front of a group.

▶3◀

Persuasion and Organization

The best speech a salesman can deliver is one that says all that should be, but not all that could be, said.
—S. H. Simmons

You may call a presentation by any name you wish: peer review, show and tell, or technical presentation. The common ground of every presentation is that you have idea A or conclusion Z, and you're asking for a reaction. *There is no such thing as an "information only" presentation.* If you need no reaction such as, "I agree," "I'll consider it," "Maybe," "Terrific," "Spend more," "Spend less," why are you standing in front of a group? A sale (idea, product, service) should be the goal of every presentation.

The better organized your content, the more easily your point of view and conclusions will surface. The better organized your message, the easier it is for the listeners to react to your ideas. That is what persuasion is all about.

Some presentations require a higher degree of sell than others. A presentation that asks for new business must use plenty of persuasion. The accountant speaking to the Junior League on how to construct a long-range family budget is not counting on a windfall of new business. Yet the speaker is certainly looking for a sale (favorable reaction) such as, "What you say makes sense. Now I can see why it's important to have a family financial plan. In fact, I plan to draw one up as soon

40

as I get home!" I think you'll agree that if most of the listeners, after hearing the presentation, thought long-range financial planning was unnecessary and not worth the trouble, we would consider the accountant's presentation a failure.

So every presenter seeks to persuade. Every presentation has an action step, such as "Consider my viewpoint" or "Buy my product or service."

▶Capturing Your Ideas

There are three elements to a successful presentation: content, delivery, and visuals. Presenters spend 95 percent of their time on content. Yet few presentations are structured to be as persuasive as they could be. Why? Because of the way presenters organize their material.

Presenters usually don't start preparing until they're close to running out of time. They approach a deadline and say, "Okay, for the next two hours, I'll set everything aside and write down my ideas." Then they fill up page after page. Unfortunately, the more pages they write, the bigger the problem.

Words hide ideas. *The more words we wrap around ideas, the harder it is to see our thoughts.* Each time we want to review the ideas, we must wade through many pages. Moving the ideas around to achieve a better sequence is difficult. We can cut and paste to rearrange them, but that gets messy and cumbersome, and not very effective either.

When you try to write all your thoughts in one or two sessions, how can you be sure you've captured *all* the major ideas? Just because you've committed 100 percent of your attention doesn't mean that your mind is suddenly going to yield all the relevant ideas in one sitting. The creative process is *not* a spigot you can turn on and off.

Ideas come and go in flashes. Suddenly one hits you. You think about it for a moment, then your mind goes on to something else. An hour later you try to retrieve that gem, but it's gone! It has been said that the mind is like a sponge forever holding ideas. Not quite. The mind generates many ideas, but retains only a few. Some of the best ideas for your presentation may come while you are commuting, reading, or jogging. The point is that your insights won't come all at once—and when they pop, they may not linger for long.

So you have two problems. You try to force the ideas out in one sitting. And you hide your ideas with too many words. You need a method that captures ideas as they surface and holds them uncluttered. Here's how:

As soon as you're scheduled to make a presentation, buy a deck of three-by-five cards and put ten cards in your pocket.

Because the presentation is due, you'll start thinking about what needs to be said. Perhaps you are on a plane. Your mind will wander, and suddenly an idea for your presentation will flash. Simply reach into your pocket and pull out a card.

Now comes the tough part. Resist the temptation to write *more than one sentence on the card.* (Remember the problem— we wrap too many words around our ideas.) Just one short sentence on the card. It must be short so you won't bury the idea.

Careful. There is danger in writing phrases instead of sentences. If you write only one word or a short phrase, you may have trouble remembering what you meant. For example, your idea might be "New cardboard package resists soaking." You write on the card, "New package." Two weeks later, you'll look at the card and wonder what it means. Was it the new graphic design for the package, the reinforced corners to prevent damage, or the new water-resistant cardboard? ("New pkg. cab'd resists soaking" would have conveyed the idea.)

Don't judge the ideas as they surface. Just gather them all without worrying whether they are appropriate or where they'll fit. At this stage you welcome all the ideas your mind is willing to yield.

As the day approaches for your presentation, you need to

start *organizing* your content. If you've been using three-by-five cards, a large part of your material gathering will have been painless. You won't be facing a deadline with that panicky feeling of suddenly having to create all the ideas.

Before we discuss the best way to arrange the thoughts you've collected on the cards, let's look at the elements of a persuasive presentation. These elements will provide a framework for your ideas.

▶Structuring a Persuasive Sequence

Presentations that persuade have these elements:

1. *Background:* giving the listeners equal footing
2. *Overview:* telling it all up front
3. *Problem/need:* why the problem exists, or why there is a need
4. *Idea/solution:* your idea, and why it will solve the problem
5. *Evidence:* the proof that your idea will work or solve the problem
6. *Benefits:* the payoff, why it's worth it, or why listeners should back your idea
7. *Action:* what is needed to proceed
8. *Summary:* recapping what you said

Neither the elements nor the sequence will fit all presentations. Most of the eight elements should be the parts of most presentations. The sequence—"background" then "overview," etc.—is simply a guideline. The action or benefit step, for example, could well be a good opener. The elements are more important than the sequence.

What follows is a discussion of each element. I'm talking about presentations within your company and presentations to prospects or clients, although the examples I've used are of the former.

"I hope this turns out to be just another of Jimerson's imaginative presentations."

Drawing by Cotham; © 1982 *Chicago.*

Element 1: Background
Giving the listeners equal footing

If you talk to a small group that's knowledgeable about what you're going to present, you won't need a background step. But suppose your boss's boss, who isn't familiar with your project, drops by to hear your presentation. When it's needed, the background step might go like this:

> "A year ago I was asked to look into why product Z was having so many problems."
> "Our early findings showed that . . ."
> "At my last presentation I said . . ."

This background step should be a minute and a half to three minutes (in a fifteen- to twenty-minute presentation).

Element 2: Overview
Telling it all up front

Few presenters use an overview. Unfortunate, because an overview is a very important step. Consider these reasons:

People Are Busy

In a business presentation you have only a short time to convince people. They have not paid to be entertained by you. Some may not even like being at your presentation. They're busy; they have their own projects and problems to wrestle with. Your presentation is cutting into their time. So tell them right at the start your main points, your conclusion, and your recommendations.

Because their time is limited, some people, especially senior executives, come to a presentation for a few minutes, then leave. An overview gives even these early departers a taste of your presentation. There is always the chance that a good overview will whet their appetite and they will stay.

No Surprises

Telling listeners quickly what you're going to discuss makes them comfortable. They won't be second-guessing you or wondering about your conclusions or recommendations.

We lead orderly lives. With the exception of movies and novels, we don't like surprises. In business, we *hate* surprises. Executives are paid to manage results—not be driven by them. Nothing is more annoying than an unexpected twist at the end of a business presentation. There won't be any surprises if you tell your listeners at the start where you're going. You might also mention what you're *not* going to cover.

Reinforcement

If you use an overview, you'll be discussing your message three times: the overview, the content, the summary.

OVERVIEW EXAMPLE

If your presentation concerns the bad news that product Z is a failure, don't save the bomb until the action step. An overview for the product Z scenario might go:

> I'll be recommending bitter medicine: We must drop product Z, transfer twenty team members and lay off five. Sales have declined 20 to 30 percent in each of the last four years. The solutions we've attempted, which I will discuss in detail later, have not solved our problem. We have tried beefing up the sales force, revamping the packaging, and a 50 percent increase in advertising. Nothing has worked. Pulling out will stop our losses *now*. We're riding a lame horse while we have thoroughbreds in new products E and H, raring to go.
>
> By dropping product Z, we can reallocate funds to E or H and beat our competitors to the finish line. An independent study has

verified that our declining sales match a declining consumer willingness to use product Z.

Gentlemen, we need to bail out. This is not the *Titanic,* but we *do* have a line fouling the propellers. Unless we untangle the line now, there could be permanent damage.

Let me start by explaining the problem in detail, the solution —pulling out—and how we'll gain by doing so.

Presenters often give too little information at the beginning. For example: "Gentlemen, we're having trouble with product Z. Let me describe the problem in detail first."

The overview should last one to two minutes.

Element 3: Problem/Need
Why the problem exists, or why there is a need

You are approaching the heart of your presentation. Be sure the listeners have a good understanding of the problem or need before you launch into the next step—your idea/solution.

The more serious the problem, the more time you should spend discussing it. If you unfold a tough problem too quickly, then your next step—the idea/solution—won't have the impact it could have.

Outline all the nasty things that combine to make a problem an important one:

- the history
- how management became aware of the problem
- why it became a problem
- what the consequences are if the problem continues
- why you were assigned to correct it
- what assumptions you made about the problem
- how you sweated to untangle the mess!

Don't rely on facts and statistics alone to prove how serious the situation is. Include the pertinent numbers, of course, but also tell how the problem has affected *people*—customers, employees, etc. Make a good story out of what you've learned

about the problem. In other words, dramatize it. Set us up to
appreciate what's to come—your idea/solution.

Element 4: Idea/Solution
Your idea, and why it will solve the problem

In this step you tell your listeners:

- your solution, stated simply but completely
- why you chose the solution you did
- how practical it is
- its cost
- what makes it the best solution
- what other ideas you discarded and why
- what problems the solution may bring
- the timetable for applying the solution
- what you need to complete the project or to improve the results

The purpose of the idea/solution step is to present your
idea and the alternatives in the simplest terms. Not every presentation need discuss all of these topics. Go easy on the statistics at this stage; they come next.

Element 5: Evidence
**The proof that your idea will work
or solve the problem**

In the previous step, your appeal was largely subjective. Now
you need to back your idea/solution with evidence. Here are
some forms of evidence:

- statistics
- facts
- similar experiences
- judgment of experts

Be careful with evidence. It tends to be overdone, and to
be self-serving. Evidence, unless it's used sparingly, tends to
sound like boasting.

Fight the urge to use everything you've learned or think you've learned about the subject. If you yield to that temptation, you'll inevitably include some less-than-solid evidence along with the hard facts that convinced you in the first place. When that happens, *all* your evidence may be discounted. Or you may spend the question-and-answer period defending an unfinished bit of research, rather than furthering your idea.

Element 6: Benefits

*The payoff, why it's worth it,
or why listeners should back your idea*

We're heading for home. You can loosen up and use all the persuasive power you have.

Most presenters spend too little time on benefits. That's wrong, because benefits are what the audience most wants to hear. *Evidence favors the presenter; benefits favor the listeners.*

Then why do presenters neglect benefits? Perhaps because it's so easy to confuse a "feature" and a "benefit." A feature statement: "Everything that goes into product E will be manufactured by our company." The benefit statement: "We can guarantee superior quality because we'll manufacture every part of product E."

If you think you have a benefit, ask yourself, after stating it, "So what?" Here are some examples of how this works.

> *Feature:* "We have 37 offices." . . . So what?
> *Benefit:* "We can provide you fast service because we have a sales/service office in every major city where you have a regional warehouse."
>
> *Feature:* "Our new plywood doesn't warp." . . . So what?
> *Benefit:* "You can store our new plywood outside and not worry about it. Your storage and packaging costs will be dramatically reduced."

Element 7: Action
What is needed to proceed

If you've been persuasive during the first six steps, the Action step should be easy. You've described the problem, how you'll solve it, and the payoff; now you're looking for a reaction. As part of your preparation, decide on what reaction you're looking for. It may be:

- an agreement to consider your idea
- an agreement to buy
- more money for your project

The point is: Ask for *something*. Don't leave the action step to the listeners. Otherwise you've rowed ten miles, then thrown your oars away on the assumption that your momentum will carry you to the dock.

Element 8: Summary
Recapping what you said

Someone once said, "Tell them what you're going to tell them. Tell them. Then tell them what you told them." Unfortunately, few follow this advice, probably because it sounds so simple. Or maybe we're so nervous when we start that we plunge in without the overview, and we're so eager to finish that we forget to summarize.

The summary is important for three reasons:

- It gives you one more chance to emphasize key points.
- It leaves the listeners with the essence of your ideas.
- It lets the listeners know you're almost finished and prepares them to be thinking of questions.

The summary should be a recap of steps 3 through 7. For example: In summary, the problem is . . . Our solution is

. . . The supporting evidence shows . . . The benefits of doing what I propose are . . . To continue we'll need. . . .

The summary should take from one to two minutes.

Framing—Reinforcing Your Points

Listeners like to know what you're going to cover. That's why listeners love overviews. So why not use an overview in every step of your presentation? I call this "framing."

You start and end every step by using an overview. For example, as you start talking about the benefits, you say, "There are three ways this will help. They are. . . ." Then you talk about each of the three in detail. At the end, you "frame" it by saying, "Now quickly, the benefits are—money, less taxes, more time off." Framing—try it. You'll raise your listeners' retention dramatically.

Now let's tie these steps and the three-by-five cards together.

Merging the Cards into the Format

You've been diligently writing three-by-five cards and thinking about the eight elements of a persuasive presentation. Sooner or later, you'll run out of either ideas or time, usually the latter. Don't panic; you're much closer to a finished presentation than you think.

Your ideas are stored on the cards. How many cards should you have? There is no fixed rule. For a twenty- to thirty-minute presentation, you may have as many as fifty or as few as ten. You may develop more as you organize your presentation.

Start organizing by labeling five blank cards with the names of five of the eight elements of the format (elements three through seven). The first card would say "problem/need"; second card, "idea/solution"; third, "evidence"; fourth, "benefits"; fifth, "action." Spread these format cards across the top of a desk or on your office floor. The cards will look like the first deal in a game of solitaire, except that your cards will be face up with the titles showing.

Now shuffle your deck of idea cards. Shuffling the cards breaks up any order they may have fallen into as you wrote your ideas. The disordering will let you test every sequence or connection between ideas.

Separate your cards by dealing each to the appropriate title card. Most decisions will be easy. You probably won't have any trouble deciding when a card belongs in the Problem or Action steps. You may have more difficulty deciding whether some cards belong with Evidence or Benefits. Don't worry about making all correct distinctions at this point.

You may even have some rejects, cards that don't fit under any of the titles. Don't feel every card has to be used. If a card doesn't fit immediately, put that card into a reject pile. When you've dealt all your cards through the first pass, go through the reject pile. After a second or third consideration, if the rejects don't fit any category, put them aside. Don't force them into this presentation. The reject pile has either irrelevant ideas— ones whose time is yet to come—or ideas that you now feel aren't as worthwhile as they seemed when they first surfaced.

Finding the Main Ideas

Let's assume you have many cards under the "problem/need" card. Look through the "problem/need" cards again. Select the ideas that are most important to describing the problem. If you have ten cards in the "problem/need" stack, there will probably be no more than two or three main ideas among them. Arrange the main-idea cards in the order that best conveys your message. Try several sequences until you find the one you like the best. Each of the remaining "problem/need" cards should support one of the main ideas.

Now focus on just the first main idea and the cards supporting it. Arrange the supporting cards in the most logical and persuasive sequence—much as you did in arranging the main ideas themselves.

Repeat the process for each main idea and its supporting cards in the "problem/need" group. Then step back and consider the result.

With luck, you will have a complete statement of the problem: main ideas that touch the important aspects of the problem, each supported by reasons and observations that your listeners will accept.

Is there enough support for each main idea? If there are gaps, you may be able to fill them on the spot by writing new cards for points that are obvious but didn't occur to you before. In some cases it won't be so easy to fill the gap. And it may be too late to gather new observations or other support. In those cases, remove that main idea from your presentation.

Repeat the process described above for each of the five elements. Next, step back and think about the sequence that best fits your content, style, and listeners. Remember, you are *not* locked into the five-element sequence. You simply want to start with this guideline, then move in any direction that your creativity and reasoning dictate.

If you have time, I recommend letting your card arrangement sit a day or so. Then come back and see if you still feel as strongly about the sequence.

Card outlining will help you grab ideas as they surface, rather than trying to force them in one sitting. Placing the cards under the format titles will help you decide if you have omissions, irrelevant thoughts, or poorly supported ideas. This system will save you time and enhance the persuasive logic of your presentation.

▶Rehearsing

After you've organized your presentation, it's wise to rehearse how your ideas sound before you create any visuals. Ideas can come across very differently when spoken than on paper. That's why so many "read" speeches sound stilted and not conversational.

For any rehearsal, *don't create a script* from your three-by-five cards. This first rehearsal is simply to see how each major point *sounds.* Go into a conference room. Study the card that contains your first major point. Then stand at the head of the table and talk. By *talking* your way through the first rehearsal, you can quickly run through three or four ways to express each major point. You're best off the cuff, so forget a script. All you need are the cards containing your major and minor points.

I know that many presenters write a script for a rehearsal. This is a big mistake. It takes time to write a script, and you end up with only *one* approach. You'll try to memorize what you've written. Not only is memorizing time-consuming, but you'll end up reading more of the script than you'll ever memorize. And you'll always keep looking at the script. The script will be a terrible crutch that keeps getting in your way each time you pause to find your place. Just tell yourself how great you are in conversation and that a script is a waste of time and a troublemaker.

Remember, this first run-through is simply to see if your ideas *sound* as good as they look on the cards. Once your sequence sounds right, think about how long your presentation needs to be.

▶How Long Can One Be Persuasive?

The secret of being a bore is to tell everything.—Voltaire

During the seventeenth century, church services lasted two to three hours. The length of Sunday messages has declined ever since. Today the average sermon is about fifteen minutes. The explanation is that after fifteen minutes "you've saved all the sinners you're gonna get." Business presenters would be wise to heed this advice.

Fifteen to forty minutes is plenty for most presentations. There ought to be some well-thought-out reasons why you need to continue for more than forty minutes. There are few legitimate ones.

Too many consultants spend a couple of hours throwing information on a screen, hoping something sticks in the listener's mind. Instead of cutting information, they try to show it all. That's one reason so many laundry-list slides are used. This "dump" type of presentation is a sure sign of poor organization.

Consultants aren't the only guilty ones. Most presentations are 10 to 30 percent too long. Too long can be only a few minutes. A good twenty-minute presentation might have been made excellent by pruning five minutes.

Covering the ground in a short amount of time gives your content more punch and impact. Your presentation needn't be as tight as the Gettysburg Address, but brevity in a presentation is almost always a plus.

It takes a real pro, however, to weed a presentation. Few of us are natural pruners, for an obvious reason. All the information we've gathered seems relevant because *we've* created it, and it looks super-relevant once we write it or see it on a slide.

Creating information is easy. Choosing not to use it is hard. Any fool can stand up and ramble. Our task as presenters is to take all we know about a subject, which can be a lifetime's worth or an hour's and present *only* the nuggets.

Copywriters have a good trick for selecting what sparkles. They write several hundred words, then lop off the beginning, on the assumption that the first few sentences are the warm-up, which lacks the snap of later copy.

Elegantly-dressed businesswomen, I'm told, do the same after dressing. They stand in front of a mirror and shed at least one piece of jewelry, knowing that at first they sometimes don one eye-catcher too many.

In a presentation, the first place to look for fat is your lead-in. My experience in working with executives is that their warm-ups, introductions, or lead-ins are often too long.

Starting a presentation with the entrée is usually better than fooling around with a tray of hors d'oeuvres. Skip "Good morning, it's nice to be here again," or "It's such an honor. . . ." Start with a long pause, then go right to the heart of your message with an attention grabber, like "The biggest problem we face . . ." or "Are you prepared to . . ." or "Dig deep, because tomorrow's. . . ."

Another fertile area for cuts is the "laundry list." If you have eight reasons why computer X is worth buying, you should probably trim them to three or five. Make your points and move on.

The danger is that we create too much. Rarely is a presentation faulted for being too lean. To achieve brevity, you'll need a *very* open mind and an unbiased sounding board. This sounding board shouldn't be afraid to tell you:

- Your logic is flawed.
- You haven't supported what you first said.
- And most important, it seems too long.

"I was up till all hours fiddling with this speech, so I sure hope you'll like it."

Drawing by Sempe; © 1980 The New Yorker Magazine, Inc.

▶Using Humor

With the fearful strain that is on me night and day, if I did not laugh I should die.—Abraham Lincoln

Humor is not used enough in presentations. Since presentations tend to be such serious matters, presenters often overlook the lighter side. Deadlines, pressure, judgment, nervousness, all seem to shape a presentation into the stiffness of a graveside eulogy.

During rehearsals, I have to continually remind executives to loosen up and smile. They unwind when I tell them they've talked for ten minutes and appear so serious that the formality could be cut with a knife.

Then there is the group that believes every presentation must start with a joke. Their feeling is that it will loosen up everyone. My advice on humor is that every presentation needs it, but not up front and only if you're comfortable with it.

Humor is like gestures—it helps to support and drive home your message. However, ten presenters, hands out of pockets, in correct stances, will have different gestures and use them in varying frequency. Humor should be the same way. The more aggressive you are, the more humor you'll tend to use. If you're on the shy side, you'll have to dig a little harder to weave some humor into your presentation.

However, don't start with humor. Nothing is more deadly than an opening line or joke that prompts silence. Your first few minutes are tough enough without also having to juggle the timing of a punch line.

An opening joke is often received only half-heartedly because the listeners are adjusting to the presenter's style and message. The same humor five minutes later will have twice the impact.

For example, let's say you're a financial officer discussing the benefits of buying government securities. I would not recommend that your opener be "Let me tell you why Fanny Mae is better than Fanne Foxe." I love the line, but I wouldn't chance it up front. Get to know the group. See how they're reacting, then go with something like, "Now let's discuss the finer points between Fanny Mae and Fanne Foxe."

I said that beyond all else the presenter must feel comfortable with humor. If you think the Fanny Mae/Fanne Foxe line is too risqué for a group of mortgage bankers, don't trot it out. It was an instant success in the presentation I heard, but that's beside the point.

If you're the slightest bit squeamish with humor, don't use it. But do search for a little lightness you are comfortable with. Humor, like good visuals, can help cast you as exciting, worth hearing, worth buying from.

►4◄

Visuals

Visual impressions are like that cannon ball; they come with a terrific impact. They imbed themselves. They stick.
—Dale Carnegie

Presenters are all too aware of nervous energy and the trouble it causes. But most presenters never realize the possible pitfalls of visuals or their absence. Two problems. First, can you get away without visuals? Second, what's a "wrong" visual?

►No Visuals

When you choose not to use visuals you'd better have three aces: a short message, stimulating content, and a very lively delivery style. Listening to a "talking head" for thirty, forty, fifty minutes is almost always a dull affair. The fast-moving action of television and movies is our visual standard. Consider that the average high-school graduate has watched 15,000 hours of television. And don't forget the astronomical number of advertisements (billboards, newspapers, magazines). We are a picture-oriented society.

I am not saying a successful presentation must have visuals. I *am* saying that without visuals it is more difficult to sell your ideas. A presenter who doesn't use visuals must work extra hard to shorten the message and put his or her heart and soul into the delivery. Without brevity and pizzazz, a presentation with no visuals is a sure loser.

▶The Wrong Visuals

If the first slide or overhead projected on the screen contains a lot of words or numbers, the viewer can be pretty sure the presentation will be a tedious one.

What do presenters do when a word/number visual appears on the screen? They read the slide aloud, verbatim, to the group. That's insulting. Listeners can read it silently much faster.

If a visual can't make the point better than the presenter, why use it?

Three reasons are often trotted out in defense of word/ number visuals:

- *Retention.* Words or numbers on a visual help the listener remember a message.
- *Simplification.* Key phrases or numbers clarify ideas.
- *Interest.* Listeners like to see words and numbers.

On pages 62 and 63 are three typical word-number creations. My goal is to convince you that these types of visuals are fraught with problems. Let's examine the above categories as each applies to word/number visuals.

Retention

Words and figures are an everyday part of business. Unfortunately, our minds don't store them well. They leave but a fleeting impression.

Scientists are not exactly sure how our minds retain information. Some believe it's coded by a chemical process, others feel it's by electrical impulses. But all researchers agree on one

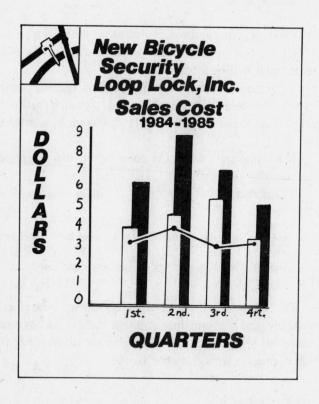

Wrong Word/Number Visuals

By permission of Loop-Lock, Inc., Wheaton, Ill.

New Bicycle Security Loop Lock, Inc.

BENEFITS

- **LOCKS/UNLOCKS IN SECONDS.**
- **BECOMES PART OF THE BIKE.**
- **COMPACT AND STRONG.**

New Bicycle Security Loop Lock, Inc.

Material Cost

Item	Per Thousand						
	1	2	3	4	5	6	7
Castings	143	167	242	264	309	336	420
Shackles	110	132	164	238	240	367	411
Locks	32	56	119	140	183	195	267
Cables	67	73	99	124	151	177	200

"Frankly, Harold, you're beginning to bore everyone with your statistics."

Drawing by Levin; © 1983 The New Yorker Magazine, Inc.

point. The mind—by retaining it longer—favors information shown as pictures. The mind quickly forgets information shown as words or numbers. Consider:

- Many more people remember buildings and vivid scenery than recall street names and addresses.
- Poems or play lines are tough to memorize, and quickly forgotten.
- Generally, faces are remembered. Names fade fast.
- We remember whole scenes from movies, but have trouble reciting more than a couple of lines.
- We dream in pictures, not words.

Thirty years ago the directions for emergency airline procedures, found in the seat pockets of planes, were 90 percent words and 10 percent pictures. Today they're 95 percent pictures. Why? Research showed that *with pictures* the passenger could very quickly understand the message and remember it longer. I assume you want the same for your presentations.

Why do so many executives use word/number visuals when they will be quickly forgotten? They throw thirty to forty of these visuals on a screen, firmly believing they will help reinforce their message.

Here is the ultimate test to determine for yourself whether word/number visuals will be remembered. *(If you try only one thing in this book, try this.)* After a presentation, corral a few friendly listeners, hand them each a pad of paper, and ask them to draw every visual that was shown. That means *all* the words and numbers on *every* slide or overhead. (Be careful about picking people who are already familiar with the content. You would expect their retention to be much higher than that of clients or prospects who would see and hear the information for the first time.)

How much do you expect your volunteers to remember? If there are over ten visuals, and they are mostly words or numbers, *your volunteers will not remember even 5 percent of each visual. Try it.*

Don't forget that they *just finished seeing* the information. Their memory is as strong as it will ever be! The sad fact is that, when you use words or numbers on visuals, the viewer's retention is practically nil. Try this same test two weeks later and you'll find the recall is less than 1 percent!

You don't believe me? You've forgotten how tough it is for the mind to digest and store words and numbers. Here are just forty-nine words, beautifully written, so reading them will be easy.

> *I returned, and saw under the sun, that the race is not to the swift, nor the battle to the strong, neither yet bread to the wise, nor yet riches to men of understanding, nor yet favour to men of skill; but time and chance happeneth to them all.*—Ecclesiastes

Quick—memorize this paragraph. How long will it take—one minute, five, ten? Now tackle the hundred-plus words and numbers on thirty to fifty overheads or slides. Impossible, right? No matter how important the presentation, viewers don't care to pigeonhole that much data.

Let's move to the argument that word/number visuals simplify a message.

Simplification

You're at your favorite restaurant with a trusted friend. You've recently invented a new bicycle lock that is permanently attached to the bike and operates in seconds. After two chocolate éclairs and three stingers, you're feeling so good you decide to tell him about your invention. You quickly explain how this neat lock works. But your friend doesn't quite grasp your idea. Waving your hands frantically, you describe it again. Still he gives you a glazed look. Frustrated, you grab the napkin and begin drawing while saying "The shackle fits into this. . . ." Of course, in reality, you don't write words; you *draw* a picture of what is churning in your mind.

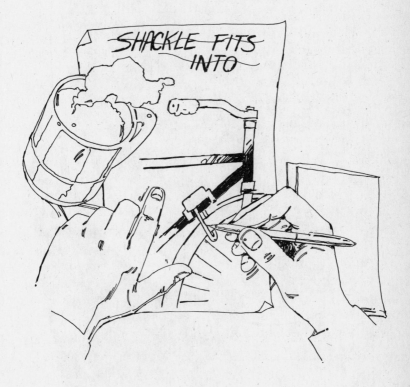

Bicycle Lock

TIME Chart by Renée Klein

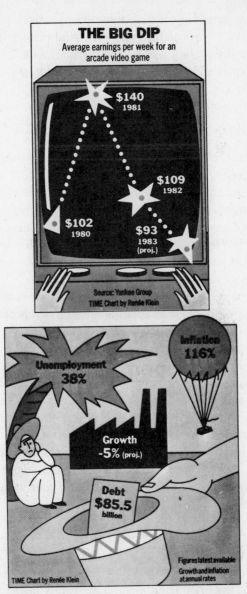

From "Wall Street's Spring Rally," "Losses and Layoffs at Atari," and "Mexico Tightens Its Belt." Copyright 1983 Time Inc. All rights reserved. Reprinted by permission from TIME..

In conversation, when we want to emphasize a point, we're likely to say, "Now picture this . . ." And pictorial terms are the key to the staying power of clichés: sly as a fox, a can of worms, apples and oranges, the bottom line, deep as the ocean, blue as the sky.

Interest

What about the last argument? Listeners prefer words and numbers as visuals.

No executive ever got invited to an art gallery to display or sell a word/number visual. But let's be more pragmatic.

Notice how the economic, financial, and statistical data are displayed in *Time* magazine. Oil-import figures become parts of an oil rig or a sheik at a gas pump. There are few naked numbers. They're all wrapped into "pictographs."

Why do you think so many *US* and *People* magazines are sold? Yes, we like to read about famous or rich people, but it's the picture format that sells these magazines.

The next time you pick up *Fortune* magazine, note that many of the lead articles are introduced with cartoon figures. These visuals draw the reader into the article. The humorous drawings and other pictures are one reason this business magazine is so widely read. Its readers, of course, include many of the senior decision makers of corporate America.

Pictorial visuals are part of what makes a home-run presentation. Lifeless word/number visuals only trigger yawns—and even a feeling of resentment. Turning your ideas into pictures gives 'them life, color, and substance.

▶Converting Ideas to Pictures

If you use the organizing method explained in the preceding chapter, converting ideas to pictures is easy. The first step is to take each three-by-five card on which you've written a com-

A meeting
should be
a controlled
situation,
not a free-
for-all.

MANAGEMENT/ANDREW S. GROVE

HOW (AND WHY) TO RUN A MEETING

ANDREW S. GROVE *is pres-
ident of Intel Corp., a
fast-growing maker of
microprocessors and com-
puter memory devices
(1982 sales: $900 million)
renowned for good man-
agement. This article is
adapted from Grove's
forthcoming book* High
Output Management.

■ Meetings have a bad name. Indeed, one school of thought considers them the curse of the manager's existence. Management guru Peter Drucker has said that a manager's spending more than 25% of his time in meetings is a sign of "malorganization." But there is, I submit, another way to regard meetings.

Meetings are nothing less than the medium through which managerial work is performed. Think about it. A big part of what a manager does is to pass along information and to impart a sense of the preferred method of handling things—"how we do things here at XYZ Corp."—to the people under him. He also makes decisions and helps others make them. Both these managerial tasks require person-to-person encounters—meetings, in short. We should not be fighting their

existence, but rather using the time spent in them as efficiently as possible.

Economics dictates as much. It's estimated that the dollar cost of a manager's time, including overhead allotted to it, is around $100 per hour. A meeting attended by ten managers for two hours thus costs the company $2,000. Most expenditures of $2,000—such as buying a copying machine or making a transatlantic trip—have to be approved in advance by senior people, yet a manager can call a meeting and

commit $2,000 worth of managerial resources on a whim. If that meeting is unnecessary or so poorly run that it achieves nothing, that's $2,000 wasted.

Be clear about the nature of a meeting. The two basic types of managerial task—passing along information and making decisions—entail two different kinds of meetings. In what I call *process-oriented* meetings—they're part of, and further, the process of managing—information is exchanged

ILLUSTRATIONS BY BILL CHARMATZ

plete sentence, and convert the sentence into a few key words. For example, your first Benefits card says, "Master inventory system is tailored to five warehouse inventory systems." You decide that the key idea is "tailored" and write it at the bottom.

Your second Benefits card says, "System produces a summary report." The key phase is "summary report." So write "summary report" on the bottom of the card.

Your last Benefits card says, "System reduces inventory shrinkage by 20%." The key thought is "a 20% savings." So "20% savings" is written at the bottom.

Most presenters will turn these ideas into one word/number slide that looks like this:

Benefits

- Our master inventory system is tailored to your five warehouses.
- Our system provides a summary report.
- Our system reduces inventory shrinkage by 20%.

In school, did you ever play that game of writing funny captions for advertisements, pictures of politicians, or famous historical figures? It's always good for laughs. People make money putting together books of pictures and captions with this sort of humor. Converting words or ideas to pictures is the same creative process. It's not difficult. With a little brainstorming, you can think of many visuals for any word or thought. Let's turn the three word ideas in the Benefits slide into pictures.

Three-by-five Card with Visual Idea

Tailored—surely an easy one. The picture of a little old tailor with his tape measure and pincushion should come to mind quickly. But let's be more creative and tie in the tailor to the "five warehouses." How about the tailor with a tape measure around the five warehouses? At the bottom of the card after the key word, "tailored," we write "tailor, tape measure, five warehouses."

Summary report—a little harder. How about showing a large stack of papers next to a small stack? We'll show the contrast between our competitor's big, bulky report and, by comparison, our thinner summary report. After "summary report" we write, "One high, one low pile of papers."

20 percent savings—now for the 20 percent. Here is a case where the number is important, so we'll use it. But we'll soften the harshness of a naked number.

You know that shrubbery around a house makes a piece

of property attractive. Trees and shrubs break the lines of the house. The house without the shrubbery is a sharp, harsh rectangle.

We can soften the number by superimposing "20" on the side of a warehouse. If we're even gutsier and want to tie 20 percent to the idea of less theft or shrinkage, we might go with a tight T-shirt squeezing a burglar. We'd put "20%" on the T-shirt. Tasteful humor as in *Fortune* magazine is always a hit, so let's use the burglar idea.

The three drawings might look like those shown on pages 75–76. Compare them to the original word/number Benefits slide.

Benefits

- Our master inventory system is tailored to your five warehouses.
- Our system provides a summary report.
- Our system reduces inventory shrinkage by 20%.

Are you satisfied with the pictorial visuals you've come up with but wonder how your clients or prospects will react to them?

Ask yourself, "Does the picture represent my concept, does it have impact, is it appropriate, is it tasteful?" If you answer "yes" to these questions, you have no problem. Your clients and prospects have tastes and lifestyles similar to yours. (They, like you, read *Time* and *Fortune* and like humor.) If you like these pictorial visuals, so will they. What's appropriate for you in a presentation most likely will be appropriate for your clients and prospects. Don't figure that, although you like them, the rest of the world prefers piles of words and numbers.

As a viewer, which presentation would you prefer to sit

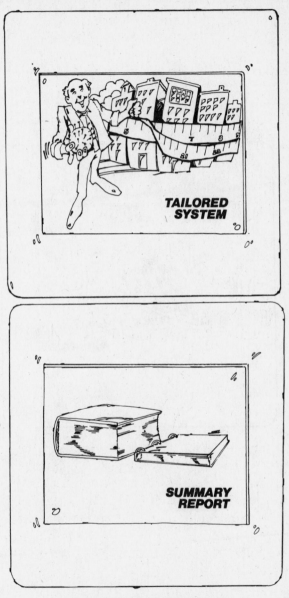

Corrected Word/Number Visuals

Corrected Word/Number Visuals

through—thirty word/number visuals or the tailor, papers, burglar type of visuals? As a viewer, which type of visual would hold your interest more? Which type of visual would you remember longer?

Which presentation would you prefer to give? Can you imagine trying to breathe life into thirty word/number visuals against a competitor who's using the tailor, papers, burglar visuals?

A presentation is a two-way street. The more favorably the listeners react—smiling, nodding—the more the presenter responds with confidence and enthusiasm. Pictorial visuals are an excellent way to stimulate viewers.

Major Ideas

Using pictorial visuals compels you to focus on your major concepts. In a presentation there are only a few important ideas; the rest is introduction, reasoning, supporting data, refuting objections, or points of secondary interest. Creating pictorial visuals is a filtering process that forces the presenter to separate the key ideas from the non-essentials. When you look at pencil sketches of your visuals, you may quickly realize that an illustrated point might be only a minor one that doesn't warrant a visual. Essential concepts, once they're expressed in pictures, will stand out. Uncluttered by accessories, your main concepts will be easily understood and remembered.

Presenters who use word/number visuals have no filtering process. They throw on the screen a ton of words and numbers on the false assumption that "the more information, the better." They end up showing so much data that they seriously dilute their main ideas. Listeners want concepts and conclusions; the nitty-gritty and supporting facts can be distributed as handouts after your presentation.

Let's look at another example—a banker showing us how to spot a company's financial weakness. You can bet the first

PE RATIO

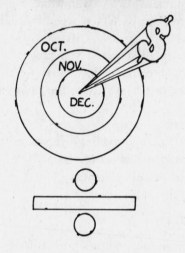

Price Earnings = **Market Value at YE**
       Ratio   **EPS**

Right/Wrong Financial Ratio

CURRENT RATIO

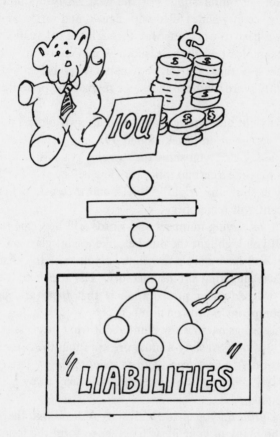

Current Ratio = Current Assets
Current Liabilities

Right/Wrong Financial Ratio

slide will be a balance sheet filled with words and small numbers. Not very interesting. For the next thirty minutes, we'll probably see fifty slides filled with figures and ratios, and we'll be shown how to work our way through the calculations. The math examples on all these slides would make an excellent handout, but they are lousy visuals. After being forced to watch fifty word/number slides, we're glad the presentation is over.

The right and wrong ways to create two typical financial visuals were seen on pages 78 and 79.

If, a day after you show the "wrong" visuals, you ask the viewers to recite a certain ratio, very few will be able to tell you. But if you show the "right" visuals, and then ask, better than 80 percent will remember.

I'm not saying numbers and words will never be remembered. If you highlight the number, like the burglar and the 20 percent, and have only a few figures, you raise the chance of these facts lingering in the memory. The problem with the typical word/number presentation is that there are just too many competing words or numbers.

This brings me to a key point about what listeners remember. In a twenty- to sixty-minute presentation, the listener will remember *only a few ideas—four to six at the most.* Even if you throw sixty slides up, the viewer still will carry away only four to six points.

The problem you create with sixty slides is that the viewer will lump many of your ideas together to form the four to six points. These points will form a hazy image at best, and will be quickly forgotten. Who has the time or the desire to file away the information on sixty word/number visuals!

I recently witnessed a fiasco in which a major engineering firm downed the lights and clicked off ninety-some slides in forty minutes. Afterward, the presenter remarked how well he thought he had sold his ideas. I told him that he had put on a good show about buildings, facts, and statistics, but that I doubted his presentation would leave his listeners with warm feelings about the capabilities of his engineers or his firm. Sure enough—his company was cut after the first round of presentations.

▶How Many Visuals?

How many visuals should you create? Hard to answer, but one good rule is that a presentation should not average more than one visual per minute. The most slides you'll need for a twenty-minute presentation, then, are twenty.

Having thirty to fifty slides for a twenty-minute presentation is a sure sign of poor organization that has led to an information dump that will never be remembered.

▶Your First Visual

Your first visual should be a title slide. For example, if you were making a presentation to Caterpillar Tractor Company, your title slide might be a drawing of the front of a bulldozer. Etched in the steel of the dozer scoop would be the words "Presentation to Caterpillar Tractor Company."

A personalized title slide immediately says to the viewers, "This presentation was created just for you. It's not a canned preparation." Title slides can be personalized by using the prospect's product, service, or logo.

A title slide has two purposes. First, it is used for focusing. As you're setting up, everyone will be watching what you are doing. The moment you project a slide for focusing, the attention will move to the screen. If you don't have a title slide, you'll be showing part of your presentation before you intended to. Second, the title slide serves as visual background for the words "The purpose of this morning's presentation is to. . . ."

If you use poster boards, and you're in a competitive presentation, try leaving your title board in the front but over to

"That's what I like about Hepworth. He keeps his presentations simple."

Drawing by Cotham; © 1982 *Chicago,* November 1982.

Title Visual

the side when you depart. It's a nice reminder while your competitors are presenting. They probably won't risk asking that it be removed. If they've used all word/number visuals, you'll really be in luck. The artwork on your title board will continually remind the viewers how much more personal and interesting your presentation was.

Your Second Visual

An agenda visual comes second. This visual may be mostly words—God willing, the *only* one in your entire presentation! The agenda visual makes the viewers comfortable because it tells them quickly what you're going to cover. It gives the immediate impression that you have an orderly, well-thought-out message. Be sure to use only key words, not full sentences. After covering the agenda visual, mention how long your presentation will be. Again, you're making the point that you've planned this presentation, rehearsed it, and know exactly how long it takes (not including questions and discussion).

▶If You're Not Convinced . . .

Before I end this section with more samples of pictorial visuals, I want to try to shake any lingering doubt you have. You might still be jittery about using visuals that I call pictorial and you call cartoons.

Pictorial visuals work. They often work in competitive presentations simply because they are different. Forget for a moment that pictorial visuals convey a better message; think only about how they set your presentation apart from the typical word/number variety.

You're the chief executive officer. Your time is important. You have three meetings in two cities to attend this week, and you still must generate a few ideas to deliver as one of the after-

Agenda Visual

dinner speakers for Friday's big civic gathering. It's Monday. Your committee is hearing three final accounting-firm presentations. The committee you chair must pick one of these firms as your new auditors. Last year's audit fee was $680,000. Each of these firms has already submitted written proposals that averaged two hundred pages. Two weeks ago you lugged the three proposals with you on a flight to the West Coast. Within an hour you had fallen asleep, bored from wading through such verbose writing—long sentences, heavy words, and very dull. After lunch you gave up, figuring that it is people you are buying, so you could decide whom to pick from the oral presentations. With relief, you went back to reading the *Wall Street Journal.*

The first presentation started sharply at 9:00. It was exactly what you expected. Five well-dressed accountants talking through thirty-six chart boards that had the key words, phrases, and numbers to remind you why they are the biggest, brightest, and best. They were allotted one hour, but with questions the darned thing took until 11:15.

After lunch the 1:30 firm started. It was an exact repeat of the morning performance. At 3:30 you were groggy. Most of the second presentation had been in a darkened room as you watched forty-seven word/number slides also reiterating why *this* firm was the biggest, brightest, and best.

Four o'clock and one more to go. With as much enthusiasm as you could summon, you waved in the 4:00 presentation.

You could hardly believe it—the partner in charge stood, pressed the clicker, and on the screen was a humorous picture of five accountants milling around a door with your company's name on it. The partner said:

Well, I'm sure you've heard a great deal about accounting today. Yes, we're also here to tell you about our services, but there is no need to bore you in the process. We've taken a different approach, because *we are different.* We thought quite a lot about these differences and would like to take only the next twenty minutes to describe how we can help you.

Competing Accountants

You could barely wait for the next slide. Maybe it's a joke! Maybe this firm has gone off the deep end. Or maybe this accountant *does* have a heart, a sense of humor, a taste for Dom Perignon. . . . Fourteen slides later, you're still wide awake. . . . "What a change. I wish my people could present like that. But those visuals! This is incredible. Different, and a bit on the gutsy side, but they sure hit the points."

Two weeks later . . . "Well, gentlemen, this is it. Today we must choose which firm we'll recommend to the directors" . . . Discussion. "Yes, Bill?" "I think the last firm gets my vote; they understand the forms problem we have in accounts receivable. Remember that visual with all that paperwork wrapped around our Atlantic warehouse. . . ."

▶Samples of Pictorial Visuals

What I've just described is very close to many situations. Starting on the next page are some visuals we've created for those who had the nerve to shoot for the bull's eye.

Summary

I don't believe that I ever had any doubts whatever concerning the salient points of the dream, for those points are of such a nature that they are pictures, *and pictures can be remembered, when they are vivid, much better than one can remember remarks and unconcreted facts.*
—Mark Twain

Visuals are so important in selling to a group that I hope you'll review these main points:

- A presentation without visuals must be brief, persuasively organized, and delivered with plenty of enthusiasm.
- Word/number visuals dull the senses, dilute main ideas, and are forgotten quickly.

Examples of Pictorial Visuals

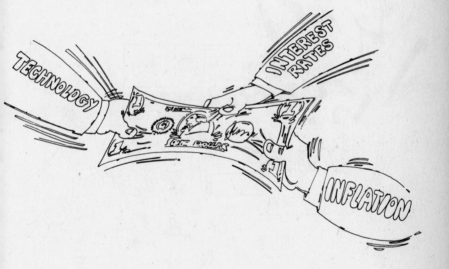

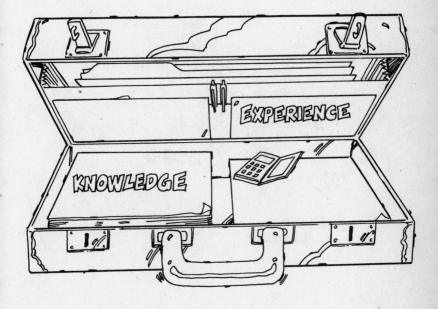

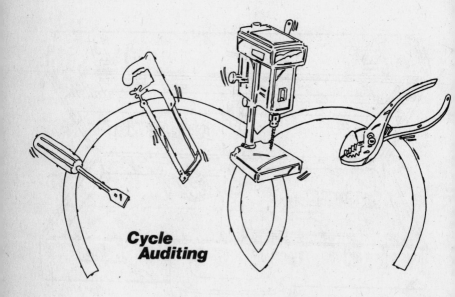

Cycle
Auditing

INVENTORY
OUT-RACES
SALES

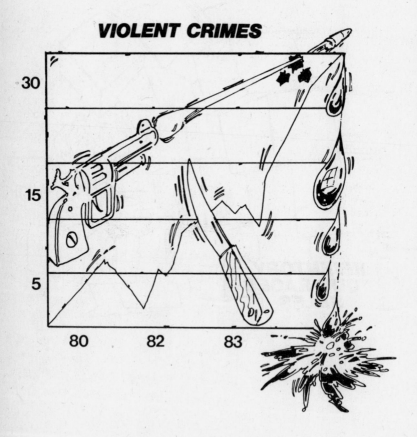

VIOLENT CRIMES

- Pictorial visuals emphasize major ideas and help listeners retain key information.
- Data are for handouts; ideas are for presentations.

▶ Artwork for Your Visuals

There are several sources for artwork: you, your staff or communications department, art teachers, freelance artists, designers, sign painters, and advertising or specialty firms.

Your Staff

If you don't draw—and most of us can't—you might discover someone in your office who does. There are plenty of latent artists outside the art world. These co-workers might be flattered that you want to use their artistic talents.

Company Artist

This inside source can be in the graphics department, PR department, advertising department, or communications department.

Art Teachers

Most grade and high schools have art teachers. Just go see them at your local school. Be careful about pushing them on tight deadlines and rush jobs and asking for a lot of changes. They may have left the art business for teaching because of such pressures.

Freelance Artists

You can find them in the phone book under "Illustrators," or ask your local art league for some names. If they're just starting, they're usually hungry for business and eager to work with you.

Sign Painters

If your artist is great with illustrations but a bit shaky with lettering, have a sign painter complete the lettering. These people are listed in the yellow pages under "Signs."

Advertising Firms

Advertising firms employ illustrators. A small firm's workload can have some valleys. However, if they're busy, they will probably turn you down, since they don't want the extra headaches.

Designers

If you want to ensure that your visuals have an extra polish, hire a designer and let him or her be responsible for selecting the illustrator. Hiring a designer will slightly increase the cost of your visuals, but it can be well worth it. A designer will also reduce your headaches and save you some errand running.

What does a designer do? Take a look at any annual report and you can appreciate what a graphic designer does. They decide if the visuals will be photographs or illustrations, choose the size and style of the lettering, and determine which visuals go on which page and how large the visuals should be so that an annual report has a theme and continuity and doesn't look like a scrapbook.

Designers can help you decide whether your slides should

be in color or black and white, and how "finished" the artwork should be. They can be responsible for rejecting or accepting the artwork before bringing it to you for approval.

You can locate designers by the same process I described for locating artists—yellow pages, art league, etc.

Specialty Firms

There are firms that specialize in television interviewing, speech writing, meeting coordinating, video-script writing or multi-media presentations. You name a communications need, and you'll find a business out there. My firm, for example, specializes in formal training, consulting, and graphic support for competitive or major business presentations.

Creating Slides

To turn your artwork into slides, you have four choices: let your designer handle it, give the artwork to a photographer, take the pictures yourself, or send the artwork to a commercial lab that will photograph it as well as process the film.

▶Choosing the Right Medium

The five most popular media for business presentations are overhead projections, flip charts, slides, poster boards, and props. Among the five are a winner, three acceptables and a big loser. I'll start with the loser—the overhead.

Overhead Projectors

Overhead transparencies have two advantages: They are inexpensive and can be made very quickly. At first that may seem like two *big* advantages. The problem is that, because of these advantages, presenters use the overhead to create and deliver the worst possible presentations.

Overhead presentations are usually copies of printed pages. The transparency becomes a sheet of sentences. Or the presenters will draw small so that they can fit fifty bars and thirty supporting numbers into a graph. Transparencies are inexpensive, quick—and dull. The overhead almost always means word/number visuals. An overhead presentation is usually an information dump.

There are other problems. I've never seen an overhead presentation where the presenters didn't deliver at least half their messages looking down into the transparencies on the machine. The equipment receives all the eye contact! The overhead arm blocks the view of at least one listener. Presenters usually stand beside the projector rather than by the screen, where they should be. Awful.

I could go on and on. Warning: The overhead projector is the worst way to sell your ideas.

Flip Charts

Flip charts are best for internal meetings; they tend to be informal and have their place in small groups. One reason I am not crazy about them is that artwork done on a flip chart is hard to preserve. The chart paper gets torn, dirty, or wrinkled.

Slides

I favor slide presentations. With slides you avoid the inherent pitfalls of the overhead—standing by the machine, talking down to the transparencies, and jabbering away while changing the visuals. With slides you're not tied to the equipment, and you have much more control over the visuals. Slides, stored out of the light, can be kept three to five years before the colors fade.

Pictorial visuals on slides mean something planned, something creative, something tailored. An effective slide presentation takes time to produce and is relatively expensive. Viewers know that, and whatever else your presentation says, slides imply, "The viewers are important enough for this effort."

Some argue that a slide presentation can be too formal or appear canned. Very true when you use word/number visuals. Not true when you use pictorial visuals—especially when you customize your pictorial visuals to include your prospect's logo, product, or service. In fact, pictorial visuals are informal enough to take the edge off the formality of a slide presentation.

Poster Boards

There are times—not many but times—when a slide presentation *is* too formal. In these situations, use poster boards.

If you're from a big city and giving a first-time, new-business presentation to an old-line, very conservative small-town company, poster boards might be more appropriate than slides.

Be careful. Boards are tricky. There is a size problem to consider, and the artwork on boards is much harder and more expensive to create than artwork for slides. In rehearsal you need to consider: Which board do you leave up? Who takes down which board? Where do you place the boards you've shown?

Props

A visual is the transposition of an idea into something one can see. So far I've implied that something as being drawn. But presenters can also use props as visuals.

Several years ago my firm worked with a company whose management wanted to change an important sales policy—a change vehemently opposed by the sales force. When it was obvious that the policy change would be made, the vice president of sales asked the directors to hold off the change for a while. He then called us to help him with the presentation he knew he must make to the board.

The sales force were asked to put in writing why they felt the change was wrong. We received many long letters all strongly opposing the change. We typed the replies and taped them end to end on butcher paper. This became a forty-foot-long sheet.

At the end of his presentation, the vice president said, "Now let me show you just how much opposition there is in the field." Then he unrolled the forty-foot paper down the board table, across the floor, and out the door into the hall.

It worked. His message was not that the policy change was so bad, but that, because there was so much field opposition, the home office would waste days and energy enforcing the change. Their efforts, he felt, could be better spent elsewhere.

One of the most effective props I ever saw was used in a courtroom. The prop was shown only during the closing remarks. The trial had been a long, heated case involving an accident that caused the plaintiff to wear a back brace.

The plaintiff's lawyer arranged to have the brace placed on a table next to him. Its cold steel and restricting straps made it an awful-looking contraption. During his thirty-minute closing arguments, the lawyer continually touched the brace and referred to the likelihood of his client's spending the rest of her life wearing that terrible brace.

He won, and I'm sure he owed his victory in part to that ugly prop.

►5◄

Staging

It has long been an axiom of mine that the little things are infinitely the most important.—Sir Arthur Conan Doyle

---

Professional service firms amaze me. They'll spend weeks pulling together an important, competitive presentation. Partners will sit around and argue over every thought and often the exact words they intend to say. Then, if they plan visuals, the decision as to which medium to use will often be made by the partner-in-charge, who knows nothing about the presentation room.

In selling to a group, one of the first considerations should be what the room looks like. Here are three short disaster stories that show why the presentation room is often "death row."

Story one

An accounting firm spends $3,000 for slides to be used at a presentation. The accountants arrive, set up the projector, and start. Then panic strikes. They're in a large corner conference room. It's a beautiful summer day with the sun blazing through two huge windows. Since there are no blinds or curtains, the slides on the screen are completely washed out—not even faintly visible.

Story two

A benefits consulting firm is in the final run-off as actuaries for a big account, so money for the presentation is no obstacle. The presenters arrive on time, but have to wait because a competitor's presentation is running late. Finally, they're ushered in and told to proceed quickly since everything is behind schedule. They unpack the projector, place it on the board table, and look for the electrical outlet. Stomachs lurch as they realize that there are only two-prong outlets. Their projector cord has a three-prong plug and they have no adapter.

Story three

An architect hates slides, so he always uses large poster boards. Besides, he argues, he needs to show a lot of engineering drawings. "With boards, I can just tape the drawings down and pass them around the conference table." (Wrong approach, but that's another story.) He doesn't like carrying an easel stand to hold the boards, so he always calls to ensure that his prospects have a stand in their conference room.

Big day arrives. Architect partner and his presentation team are greeted warmly by the executive committee and told to proceed as soon as they're ready. Embarrassment quickly spreads as the previously requested stand turns out to be an unusual easel with no ledge to hold the charts.

▶Casing the Room

The conclusion should be obvious. Inspect the presentation room before deciding whether to use slides, overheads, flip charts, or boards. Sketch the room, the table, the exact number and location of chairs, the wall switches, the screen position,

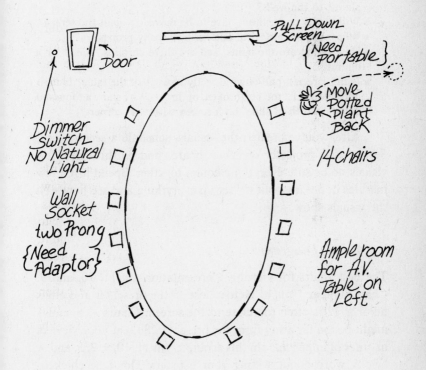

Sketch of Presentation Room

the projector's place, and the electrical outlets. Then ask yourself:

- Can chart boards or flip charts be seen adequately if the board room is long and narrow?
- Is there room for a screen and projector if the board table extends almost to the walls?
- Will plants or furniture have to be moved to slant the screen?
- Where are the electrical outlets; how many prongs?
- How bright are the lights, and are there curtains, blinds, or a dimmer?
- Is the screen a pull-down directly in front of the table? Is their portable screen too big, broken, or dirty? (Why show a thousand dollars' worth of slides on a screen with torn corners?)

After you've created the visuals, schedule a second visit. Set up your projector or poster boards and go through a few visuals, to be sure everything comes together. Spend just a few minutes doing this, but *do* set up everything and see how well the visuals show.

Room Diagram

The best chairs for viewing a presentation are 11, 10, and 9. Chair number 1 might be too close to the presenter and chair number 12 is often too close to the screen. Chairs 8, 6, and 5 might be too far away from the presenter. So seat your viewers in order of importance in this arrangement 11, 10, 9, 2, 3, and 4.

A word about seating your listeners. Don't be chicken-hearted. Yes, it's *their* board room, but it's *your* presentation —and your nice fee if you rope a sale. As you set up the projector, you should mumble to your prospect's senior member something like, "I'm going to use a slide projector, and I don't want the hot air blowing in your faces, so would C.J. sit here, Jessica sit there, etc." You are their guest, so they will be happy to accommodate you. But do this *before* everyone settles down and silence prevails.

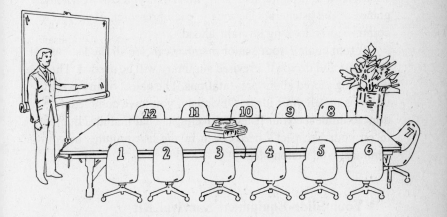

Projector on Boardroom Table

In most competitive or team presentations, your senior member will speak first and last. He or she should start by sitting in chair 1. After his or her remark, he or she takes the chair of the second presenter, 7. Chair 1 then stays empty. Your team should sit in chairs 5, 6, 7, and 8. Your senior member or leader should sit in chair 7, because from this vantage point he or she gets the best view of the listeners' reactions, facial expressions, body movements, etc. The worst chair for observing these reactions would be number 1. In this chair you can't turn and glance at the listeners' reactions to each presenter. Here you're committed to looking straight ahead.

From chair 7 your senior member can see all the listeners' reactions and decide if a revised summary will be needed. There is nothing sacred about presentations. The object of any presentation is to sell your ideas. Obviously, you have complete freedom to influence your listeners' feelings. That includes homing in on your prospect's needs even in the last minutes of your summary and action step.

▶ Your Slide-Equipment Survival Kit

A slide presentation is fraught with logistical problems. I strongly suggest that you include in your slide projector case the following items:

1. Zoom lens—102 to 152 mm, f/3.5. This lens will give you considerable flexibility to control the image size. In fact, leave this lens in your projector. The standard non-zoom lens that comes with the projector is of little use for business presentations.
2. A clicker cord extension. In a large board room you'll need the extra length.
3. An extension cord. The outlet may be out of normal cord reach.
4. Tweezers. They come in handy to remove jammed slides. Also, learn about the screw that allows you to remove the slide tray.

5. Plug adapter. You won't always find a three-prong outlet.
6. Extra projector bulb. If you don't carry one, you're a masochist. Remember, bulbs don't burn out when they're not being used.

With your projector case should go an AV (audio-visual) table. An AV table is simply a metal plate about twenty inches by twelve inches. It's quite portable. The four table legs are held by clips under the plate. To use the legs, you unclip them, screw them into the four corners and loosen the screws that allow you to telescope the legs to the table height you need. The beauty of an AV table is that it gets the projector off the board table. If the projector is on the board table, some chairs will not be worth using because of the noise and hot air from the projector fan.

If your prospect's screen isn't to your liking, bring your own. The best all-purpose screen for small-group, board-room-size presentations is sixty inches by sixty inches.

With your projector, the AV table, the screen, and your box of handouts, you'll need a camel! Don't give up; it's well worth it. And don't listen to the cronies in your office who say, "Why bother with all that—let's just sit around the table and keep it casual." These are the people our clients defeat every week.

▶The Screen—Stand Next to It

Screens seem to cause as many problems as lecterns. Presenters never question the location of either. They just step up and start "using" them.

How many presentations have you seen in which the speaker is behind the lectern on one side of the room and the screen is on the other? This is typical of annual shareholders' gatherings or large national meetings. As the speaker talks about the information on the slide, where do the listeners focus

Projector on AV Stand

their attention—on the screen or across the stage on the presenter? Their attention is divided. As slides change, the listeners move their heads and eyes back and forth like people watching a tennis match.

This divided attention weakens the message. Think about watching a foreign movie with subtitles. You don't read all the words because your main interest is watching the picture. The same happens in a split presentation. The listeners miss many of the words because they're watching the visuals.

The cure for this problem is easy. The presenter should be next to the screen. But angle the screen. In board rooms, screens are usually centered over one end of the table, causing presenters to deliver their presentations off-center. This is a mistake because the *focal point* is the screen, not the presenter.

Presenters should stand in the center at the end of the board-room table with a screen slanted to their left. Now the presenter is the focal point and the screen secondary. Remember that a visual aid is just that, an aid. It's not the show; *you* are.

The information is to the presenter's left because our eyes are used to seeing information from left to right—like reading this page. So the presenter on the left is the anchor or focal point to which the listener's vision always returns. (Refer to the illustration on p.118.)

Presenters are more important than the visuals. If the information on the screen is more important, print your message in a brochure, and sell through the mail. *Presenters are in a room to make information come alive, to give it depth and richness, meaning and credibility.* So presenters should be at the center—not the screen.

Split Presentation

▶The Lectern—Get Away from It

The lectern was originally designed to hold speakers' notes. Through the years, technical advances have done marvelous things to the simple lectern. Now we have a large, expensive oak cube that hides most of the presenter. Its elaborate control panel can dim the lights, lower the projection screen, advance the next slide, and adjust the room temperature. It has a microphone and a shelf for the speakers' water. It won't surprise me if the next generation of lecterns are built to handle the nervous presenters' need to relieve themselves.

Move the lectern just off center of a room or stage. Four feet from the right side of the lectern, place your slanting screen. The lectern is to hold the slide projector clicker and your five-by-eight cards. *Don't stand behind it!*

▶The Microphone—Disconnect It

Dismantle the mike from the lectern. That's right; you rarely need a microphone. Maybe for an audience of three hundred or more you need one, but even in hotel ballrooms you can project your voice without shouting and be heard.

There are three reasons for *not* using a microphone:

1. Projecting your voice is an excellent way to burn off nervous energy.
2. Speaking more loudly encourages natural gesturing.
3. Mikes rarely work correctly.

Projecting Your Voice to Burn Nervous Energy

Remember that I said starting eye contact in the back of the room projects your voice and keeps it from stalling. If a louder

Positioning the Lectern, Presenter, and Screen

voice benefits you at the beginning, why not receive the benefits throughout your presentation? A firm voice, like a solid handshake, shows the group you're committed to what you are saying. If they feel *you* are convinced, it's easier for them to accept what you're proposing.

Speaking More Loudly and Gesturing

Speaking loudly guarantees that you will use more gestures. Remember the last time you argued? You probably had terrific gestures—pounding your fists, waving your arms, and shaking your finger. Obviously, your self-control won't allow you to go berserk in a presentation, but a stronger voice will shake loose many gestures.

Murphy's Law and Mikes

Of course you know that "Murphy" (of "what can go wrong, does" fame) rides on both shoulders when you're selling to a group. The first trick Murphy tries is to derail the mike—it's easy to do. Because they're so temperamental, mikes rarely work well, especially during those large, important presentations. Microphone systems sound tinny; or they fade in and out; or, when you lean too close to them, they blare out a hundred decibels too loud; or they set off a high-pitched squeal that makes everyone wince. Hotel ballroom microphone systems are usually cheap ones, so your voice sounds like some uneven, squeaky noise emanating from the ceiling.

Executives sound ridiculous saying, "Testing, testing, can you hear me . . . can you hear me now?" Then they helplessly flick the mike with their fingers. Forget microphones. They never work when you need them. Projecting your voice is much better.

▶ **The Projector—Don't Block the Light Path**

In a board room or ballroom, the projector should be placed on an AV table against the extreme right side of the room—the presenter's right.

Now project your first slide. If you're in a ballroom facing three or four hundred people, you'll probably need to have the slide image fill the screen. But, if your audience is fifteen to thirty, or if you're in a board room, adjust the zoom lens to the smallest image that can be seen adequately from a chair in the back. Just because the screen is huge doesn't mean you must fill it. Don't let the visual overpower the presenter. You don't want to be a little narrator beside a giant picture. The presenter—not the information—is the show.

Be sure you don't wander into the path of the projector light. Executives look funny when the image is two-thirds on the screen and one-third on their suits and faces.

Remember, "Murphy" is trying his best to get you. So, if you step into the projector light of a slide titled "Steel Products of the Future," it will be just your luck to find the word "eel" stenciling your cheek. This will induce a ripple of chuckles—at your expense.

A few tips for the projector clicker. With a green felt-tip pen or green stick-on label, mark the "forward" button on the clicker. This will help you *not* to push the reverse button (green for "go"). Clickers often slide off the table or lectern. To prevent this, make a small loop from masking tape or double-sticky tape and place it on the underside of the clicker. Then you'll have a clicker that will not slide away.

▶The Lights—Leave Them On

Please don't turn off the lights. It's sad how many ideas are wasted in the dark. In a darkened room you forfeit the best part of a sale—you, the persuader.

If you must, dim the lights; however, you'll rarely need the dimmer. It's just a habit: show time, so we turn off the lights. Good idea for a movie theater, bad idea for selling to a group. True, the slides will be brighter in the dark, but at what a price. Slides show up adequately in a fully lit room. Sometimes closing the blinds or the curtains will be enough, or you can remove the two or three ceiling bulbs that are closest to the screen. (All these little tricks help. Our clients must agree, because in the last few years we've redesigned the lighting arrangements and screens in a dozen conference rooms.)

Just because your presentation is in a hotel ballroom, don't think you can't remove the light bulbs or have that huge lectern moved. Somebody's paying the hotel a healthy fee for the ballroom, meals, and drinks. You have every right to ask for the changes. It's your presentation, your moment to shine; don't let the hotel dictate your chances for success.

▶Stance

With visuals, presenters tend to turn *toward* the visuals and talk to the screen instead of to the listeners. Here are two tips to overcome this: (1) keep your feet pointed toward your listeners, weight distributed equally, and (2) always use your left hand for pointing.

Keeping your feet planted directly toward to the group will keep you from facing into your visuals. There is a strong tendency to shift toward the screen. You must continually remind

Right Stance at Screen

yourself to reposition your feet so you directly face the listeners.

If you point with your right hand, you will turn a half-step into your visuals. Not only will you now be facing the information, but the right side of your body also will be blocking the screen from those sitting on your right. So always point with the *left* hand. As you point to the screen, chart board, or flip chart, turn your body from the waist. Don't move your feet.

If you must use an overhead projector, stand at the screen, not at the projector. If you stand at the overhead, you'll have two problems. You'll aim your words into the transparencies, and you'll split the viewer's attention between you and the screen. Don't have someone else change your transparencies. Pause, step to the overhead, change transparencies, step back, get the eye contact, and only then start talking. The built-in pause will do wonders for your presentation.

Maybe you'd resist this, because many of your visuals will be shown for only a few seconds. If this is your reply, then I'd say there is something very wrong with your visuals.

▶When Not to Talk

Here's one of those rules that should never be broken but always is. *Never, never* talk while you're doing something physical. Don't talk while you're changing transparencies, pushing the carousel clicker, flipping the chart paper, or putting up the next chart board. The spontaneity of your delivery will be cut in half because your thoughts will be on changing the chart board, pushing the clicker, flipping the page. Your volume will drop and you will, of course, have no eye contact, since you'll be wrangling with the paper, clicker, chart, etc.

Pause, do the physical thing, reestablish eye contact, then continue talking. You'll look and sound much more professional. If you talk while you're doing something physical, your listeners will miss key words because they are watching you do

Wrong Stance at Screen

the physical task. Remember: the eye is drawn to color, noise, and movement—especially movement.

▶Visuals and Talking

When your visual hits the screen, pause two full seconds before you speak. For the first couple of seconds, a new visual will absorb almost 100 percent of the group's attention. So if the instant a slide appears you say, "This is the most important benefit because, . . ." the viewers will probably miss your key thought. Viewers require a few seconds to take in your visual before they shift gears to seeing and listening.

Press the clicker, look at the visual, pause two seconds, look back at the listeners, bore in on eye contact with only one individual, then start talking.

▶Destroying the News

After pausing, your first words should "take the news value" out of your visual. Failure to do so has its penalties. You see this mistake all the time with word/number visuals. The visual will have, say, three bullet points: "tailored system, summary report, and 20% shrinkage." The presenter starts with the first item, telling us all about the tailored system. While the presenter is talking, the listeners are also seeing the other two points. They might be thinking, "I wonder what he means by 'summary report.' Is he going to tell us we will be able to get only a few reports from these systems? . . . I sure don't want that . . . maybe it means we won't need any reports . . . no, that couldn't be! Ah, what about that 20 percent? How did he get that?"

The presenter should handle such a visual like this:

- New slide appears on screen.
- Presenter pauses and looks at visual for two seconds.
- Presenter turns back and assumes eye contact with one individual.
- Presenter moves hand in a circular motion about the three bullet points and says, "There are three benefits to our system."
- Presenter moves hand to underscore first phrase and says, "Our master inventory system is tailored to fit your five warehouses."
- Presenter moves hand to underscore second point and says, "This master system produces an executive exception report. This report doesn't bother you with a lot of nitty-gritty information."
- Presenter moves hand to underscore third point and says, "In catching mislabeled items alone, our system will reduce your inventory shrinkage by about twenty percent."
- Presenter pauses and says, "Now let's discuss each of these benefits in detail."

Because the news value has been taken out of the visual, the listener is now more likely to concentrate during the presenter's more-detailed explanation that follows. The visual then acts as a reinforcement. (A terrible one in this case, since the visual is of the word/number variety.)

Notice also that the presenter doesn't say, "This visual shows" or repeat the exact words that are on the visual. All that's needed to destroy the news value is a quick summary of the key points.

There is another benefit to quickly taking the news value out of each visual. As you go back to describe each point, you won't belabor the ideas because you've already told us the heart of each concept. Destroying the news value forces you to present your ideas more concisely and cover the points more quickly. Listeners appreciate that!

Another example: Your visual is an income sheet for a company that lost $3 million last year. Many presenters would start with a long discussion of the income and the expenses, then say, "As you can see, this company lost three million dollars."

Destroying the news value means to begin by pointing to the bottom line, saying, "This company lost three million dollars for one reason—their biggest customer reduced orders by . . . Now let me take you through the income and expenses in detail."

If you start your discussion at the top of the balance sheet, where do you think most of the listeners' attention will be? Of course, at the bottom, glued to the $3-million loss. Then viewers will start scanning the income and expense items to see why the loss occurred.

Until a viewer's curiosity about the visual is satisfied, the presenter's words will receive only half the attention. So quickly take the news value out of every visual.

▶"Massaging" the Visual

Successfully handling visual information means tying your words *to your visuals.* You cannot do this standing motionless as each visual is shown. You and the visual must come across as one message—not separately. "Massage" the visual. As you speak, point to it, leading your viewer through the information. As you discuss your idea, your left hand points to the key concepts in your visual. You may, and should, also gesture with the right.

It's not just pointing, but the hands moving, up, down, across, in slow or quick "articulate" gestures. As you describe the visual in words, your gestures help convey it with motion. It is the gestures—movements—that tie your words and the visuals together. Think how the viewers' eyes will stay riveted to the visual with this type of delivery and how they will wander away if the presenter talks while standing at parade rest.

Besides keeping the listener's attention, "massaging" the visual provides a bonus—it's an excellent way to burn off nervous energy.

►6◄

Questions, Answers, and Handouts

The presentation is over. Now most presenters think they're finished, especially if they ask, "Are there any questions?" and none come. Most presenters think that having no questions means they have covered all the bases, and the sale is wrapped up. The opposite is generally true.

Presenters need questions to gauge how near they are to closing the sale. In competitive presentations, the question-and-answer session can be as important as the presentation. Questions are so important in competitive presentations that in our consulting work we often design mini question-and-answer sessions into the format of the presentation itself. It's during the question-and-answer period that you can uncover what wasn't fully understood. Or discover what your client thought about your competitor's presentation. But to do this you need to know how to prompt questions, because questions won't always come automatically.

►Prompting Questions

Questions don't come for two reasons. First, the listeners may need time to think of them. Second, there may be a fear as to how other listeners or the presenter will react to the question.

Thinking of a Question

The presenter has been speaking for twenty minutes, then says, "Well, that's it; are there any questions?" Listeners need time to think of questions. Give the group ten or fifteen seconds to think about your message, and you'll have all the questions you want. Presenters often panic after four seconds of silence and say, "Okay, thanks," and sit down without receiving any questions.

Reaction to the Question

Questions may be slow to come because of apprehension. "How will the presenter react to my questions? Will the presenter think it's a dumb question? What will the other listeners think about my question? Is it a good question?"

These are legitimate fears. To promote questions, you must eliminate these concerns and give listeners a chance to generate a question or two.

Transition Period

At the beginning of your presentation, say whether you do, or do not, want to be interrupted by questions, and state that there will be a question-and-answer period when you finish. After your summary, say, "Okay, it's about time to answer questions, but before I do I'd like to. . . ." What follows is a transition between your formal presentation and the informality of a question-and-answer session.

Start the transition period by asking the group a question. For example, if your presentation was on why a company should fund a fitness program, your transition might be, "I'd like to ask how many of you already jog or lift weights?" The purpose of the transition period is to get the listeners thinking about questions and see that you'll handle their questions with tact and consideration.

A tip on handling the above question: Whenever you ask for a survey, feed the results back to the group. The listeners in the front cannot see the other raised hands. After you've quickly counted the hands, say, "I see about two-thirds of you already exercise on your own." Then ask a few how far they run or how often they lift weights.

You've warmed them up for questions, and you have given them a feeling of how you'll react. Now you can say, "I'd like to turn the talking over to you. Any questions?" (Pause five seconds.)

If you draw silence at this point, try a different tactic: Tell the group that, when you've given this presentation before, "the most frequently asked question has been. . . ." Then say, "Now what questions may I answer?" If you're still facing silence, try this. Pause for a full ten seconds. This technique almost guarantees questions will start. But you must have the courage to endure *silence up to ten seconds.*

While you ask, "What questions may I answer?" and you're waiting out your ten seconds, keep your hand raised. Raising your hand visually reminds the group that you're seeking questions, and it tells them how you want them to respond. If you don't raise your hand, the group won't know whether to blurt out questions or raise hands to be recognized. This small indecision alone can cause some people to hold back on questions.

▶Giving the Best Answers

As questions come, handle them in a three-step process. First, indicate which question you'll take by pointing to the person. Second, give 100 percent eye contact to the person as he or she is asking the question. You want to show that both the question and the questioner are important. Three, when the questioner finishes, pause, and repeat the question *as you move the eye contact around the group.*

Repeat the Question

Always repeat the question. If the listeners did not hear the question, they either must wait for the next question or try determining the question from the answer.

Another reason to repeat the question is to give you time to consider your answer. Many presenters undervalue this advice. What they forget is that to every question there is a right answer and an appropriate answer.

If you forget to repeat the question, you may respond with the *right* but not the *appropriate* answer. For example, you are a consultant with an accounting firm and have just finished a presentation to a company's executive committee. You proposed installing an internal-control system that would keep better track of the company's inventory levels. The first question comes from the president. He looks you right in the eye and says, "Will this new system you're touting guarantee that we won't have any more shortages in our warehouses?" If you don't buy yourself a few seconds' thinking time, your response will be something like "No, I can't guarantee that."

The response is certainly the right answer, but not the appropriate one. Repeating the question might have produced something like "The question is, can I guarantee you'll have no shortages?" Pause. "This is, after all, a system, and that makes it fallible, but it is the best inventory control system on the market. There is nothing better. That's why I recommend it. I *can guarantee* that this system will be a tremendous improvement over what you're doing now."

Repeat the heart of the question. If the question is: "Jim, you said the cost for this inventory control system will be $30,000. That's a lot of money. I happen to know there are systems on the market that are a lot cheaper. Besides, I think the cheaper systems are all we need." Your repeating his question might be, "Why do you need to buy the XYZ system?"

Should you always repeat the question? Yes, until it becomes a habit. If you don't make it a habit, you won't repeat a question in a tough spot. In presentations, nervous energy has a way of bringing out the worst in us unless we form strong habits to carry us over the rough spots.

Neutralize Negative Questions

A point on repeating the question. When a questioner asks a nice, concise question, there is nothing wrong with simply repeating the exact words. However, you can restate a question so that it comes out as negative, neutral, or positive. Example: The question, "Why are your fees so high?"

Repeated—"The question is, . . .

Negative: Why do we have high fees?"
Neutral: "Explain our fee structure."
Positive: "What is the value of our service?"

You shouldn't distort a person's question, but don't repeat it so it's stacked against you. I remember a series of seminars we were conducting for a food-processing company. A product manager was up fielding his series of questions. Suddenly, someone said, "I think your product line stinks!" In repeating the question, the product manager did a very clever thing. Obviously, there was one word he did not wish to repeat. Here's how he handled the situation. He replied: *"The quality* of our product?" Pause . . . "Independent testing repeatedly shows we have the highest quality-control standards in the food industry. Next question, please."

Nicely done, and a good example of turning a negative question into a positive answer.

Moving Eye Contact

Moving eye contact throughout the group as you repeat and answer each question is a must. Your responsibility is to the group, not just to the person asking the question. Often, one question is on the minds of several listeners. One person just had the courage to ask. By moving the eye contact while you repeat the question and answer, you involve *the group* as well as the questioner.

Watch carefully the next time you're in a question-and-answer session. Here's what usually happens: A question comes, and the presenter takes a step toward the questioner. At the end of the question, the presenter looks right at the questioner and starts spitting out the answer without repeating the question. The presenter will look at and talk mostly to the questioner.

As a listener, you certainly don't feel very involved in the question if all the eye contact is going to just one person. Besides, you were going to ask the same question, but the presenter acknowledged old Frank because he was gray at the temples and a senior vice president. So you sit back, not really caring about either the question or the answer.

Now, you're the presenter again. As you finish answering the question, you have an important choice to make with eye contact. If it's a friendly question, and you want to be sure you gave a good answer, end your eye contact on the questioner. This visually asks the questioner, "Did I give you a satisfactory answer?"

However, there is a danger in doing this. If you look back to friendly questioners, they may like your visual acknowledgment so much that they pop you another question. Remember, your responsibility is to the group. You want to spread the questions around as much as possible. If, at the end of every question, you return your eye contact to the questioner, you may be encouraging multiple questions from only a handful of listeners.

If you encounter hostile questions, you definitely don't want to return your eye contact to the questioner. You'd be asking for more. So, if you're getting hostile questions, end your eye contact on the opposite side of the room from the antagonist and quickly acknowledge the next question. Then, if the antagonist begins to throw another remark your way, he'll be interrupting a member of the group. These rude interruptions will quickly turn the listeners against the antagonist.

You need to be very careful with hostile questioners. Don't be cute or offer wisecrack remarks in return. This can quickly turn the listeners against you. Nothing rallies a group faster than a presenter who has been rude to one of its members.

Handling a Compliment

Don't be thrown by a sudden compliment in a Q-and-A session. Not all questions are loaded or negative. Let's say you're giving an architectural presentation. Your proposal involved a radical new public building design. You're answering a series of tough questions from the public-works committee. Suddenly, an official who hasn't said much pipes up with "Three years ago I was a director for the XYZ Company that hired this firm for a multimillion-dollar building complex in Kuwait; they did one hell of a great job; you can't believe the problems they had to overcome." Pause. Let the silence run for five seconds so the group taste his remarks; follow with a smile and say, "Thank you; (pause). . . . Are there any other comments?"

No "Excellent Questions" or Names

You should never compliment a questioner with "Excellent question," or "I'm glad you asked that," or "That's a well-thought-out question." Once you do this and don't compliment the next question, that person will wonder, "Isn't my question 'outstanding' or well-thought-out too."

Unless you know everybody's first name, don't call anyone

by a first name. Just "Yes" is fine. If you go around the room taking questions by saying, "Yes, Bill," "Yes, Ralph," "Yes, Jane," "Uh, yes, sir," that last person may well think, "Hey, he knew Bill, Ralph, and Jane, but he doesn't know my name, and I'm one of the decision makers!"

Short Answers Are Best

When you start your answer, be careful about excess words. For example, "In my opinion, I think that we should . . ." Eight words that say nothing. Obviously it's your "opinion," and obviously you "think."

The best answers are condensed into a few well-chosen words. Nobody wants to hear a five-hundred-word answer. You already had your chance during the presentation. Besides, the best Q-and-A sessions occur when most of the listeners voice their opinions. If you're giving long-winded answers, only a few people will have time to ask questions.

Don't Know the Answer?

You've just been asked a question that throws you. What do you do? Well, you read my next book, *Lying, Cheating, and Stealing*! Of course, you say, "Gee, I'm sorry I don't know the answer to that one. If you'll leave your business card, I'll get back to you." Be sure to add that any others interested in the answer may leave their cards, also.

Trying to fumble around and fake an answer puts everything you've covered in jeopardy. It's like having a rope around your neck and trying to step off the chair lightly. You'll occasionally get away with it, but most often you'll twist and choke in full view of your listeners. And down goes your credibility.

Summary

Here are the steps for handling a Q-and-A session.

1. Create a transition between the presentation and the Q and A.
2. Raise your hand while waiting for questions.
3. Indicate which question you'll take next by pointing to the questioner.
4. Give 100 percent eye contact to the questioner while the question is being asked.
5. Repeat the question.
6. Move the eye contact throughout the group as you repeat and answer each question.
7. As you're finishing each answer decide whether to return to the questioner to end your eye contact.

▶ Handouts—Creating Something Special

Handouts are another ball in the air. Here are a few tips so the handout won't be one juggle too many.

Directions

Take the "news value" out of a handout *before* you pass it out. It should be obvious that, once the listeners have it, the handout receives most of their attention. You'll be fighting a losing battle if you're giving directions or comments while the listener peruses the handout.

Destroying the news value includes showing each page you plan to review. Summarize each page just as you would a visual. Be sure *not* to hold the handout as you do when you read a book.

Right

Wrong

Reviewing Handout

Timing

Distribute a handout *after* your presentation, not before. Handouts distract listeners. It's the old split presentation again. The eyes move from handout to presenter, from presenter to handout. Listeners catch your message only in dribs and drabs because of the split attention you force on them.

A Visual Reminder

A *tailored* handout is easy to prepare and a terrific silent partner, reinforcing your message weeks after your presentation.

Here's how it works. Tell your artist to produce a PMT (photo-mechanical transfer, sometimes called a "stat") before adding the color to your visual. A PMT is a black-and-white photo of the drawing. With a PMT you can reproduce your drawing on any copy machine. (A colored drawing doesn't copy well.)

Under each picture include ten to a hundred words. PMTs can be made to any size, so you can have one or several of your visuals per page, plus the copy. Simply put double-sticky tape on your PMTs and the copy; arrange them on the pages and run the pages through the copier.

Handouts that include your visuals have two advantages:

- Your listeners will remember your message, because few presenters ever bother to reproduce their visuals.
- If a competitor follows your presentation, the listeners probably will start flipping through *your* handouts. This will really unnerve your competitors, who are trying desperately to get their points across!

Tailored Handout

►7◄

Special Presentations

You will never become a successful account executive unless you learn to make good presentations. —David Ogilvy

---

Most business presentations involve selling your ideas to a small group around a conference table. However, there are plenty of exceptions. You could be part of a team presentation or facing a large group in a client seminar.

Here are four special situations: team presentations, client seminars, multimedia shows, and courtrooms.

►Team Presentations

The biggest time waster in team presentations is the first meeting. The group sits around for three or four hours trying to piece together who should say what. Here is how you can save time and be much more productive.

Before your first strategy meeting, all participants need to be equally informed. Call a fifteen- to twenty-minute meeting to cover the background information. Don't attempt to do more than explain the background. After you cover the background tell the group that before the next meeting, each participant should write all major points on three-by-five cards. (See in Chapter Three, "Capturing Your Ideas"—every idea must be written in brief sentence form and only one idea per card.)

At the first strategy meeting, participants quickly summarize each of their three-by-five cards. After hearing all the major points, it's much easier to talk about which ideas are appropriate, which to expand, which to narrow, or what might be missing.

You can use these cards for another helpful step—setting the order of the topics. From each participant's cards, choose the idea that best states each major point. Lay these cards on the table. Rearrange them in the order that the group feels creates the most persuasive sequence.

Rehearsals

A team rehearsal can be another big time waster. After the strategy meetings, the group will blow a few more hours rehearsing what they intend to say.

Treat rehearsals as if team members were in front of the prospect. Don't let speakers sit and say, "What I intend to cover is. . . ." That just puts off what needs to be done—getting up on one's feet and practicing the actual words. No matter how rough, insist on this procedure even for the first run-through. Presenters will accomplish a lot more (and faster) by standing and trying what they will actually say in front of the prospect than by sitting around discussing what they intend to cover.

Some speakers decide that writing a script will help them for the rehearsal. As I explained under "Rehearsing" on page 54, scripts are not the answer and only make one's preparation harder and longer.

Rehearse as if it were the final presentation. If the slides aren't ready, practice pushing the clicker, using all the gestures and words you would if you had your slides. If you're planning to use poster boards, practice with four or five blank boards. You'll work out the bugs, such as, "Do I leave my last board up or leave the tripod empty for the next presenter? Do I say something before my next slide, or do I just pop it on the screen with no transition?"

Choosing Team Members

In choosing team members, pick the better presenters. You're selling people, not information. If you have presenters who really shake and fumble in front of a group, downplay the problem with terrific visuals—pictorial, not word/number.

Any team member who's going to be at a presentation should have some oral part. And those who will have continuous contact with the client should have major parts in the presentation. Don't arrive with just the marketers and the bosses.

When There Is Competition

Maybe you have a sensitive point—you have high fees, or your team was recently terminated from a similar engagement—and you are wrestling with whether to tell the prospect. My advice is to bring it out in the presentation; otherwise, your competitors will be sure to turn this knowledge against you. Your silence will leave important gaps for your prospect to fill in haphazardly.

Early into a consulting project, I ask a client, "What are the harshest things your competitors could say about you?" Then the positive sides of these points are included in the presentation.

It's best to be last in a series of competitive team presentations, but there is a danger. Listeners tire from four or five presentations, especially after seeing a zillion word/number visuals. So your prospect suddenly gets a little unfair and switches the rules of the game. As you're setting up, he might announce that the chairman must leave in ten minutes. Instead of the thirty minutes you were allotted, your team now has only ten.

Don't be too hard on the prospect. It's not easy to sit through five presentations; there are many other things in life more enjoyable. Getting cut short doesn't happen often, but often enough so that I recommend you give serious thought to what you would cover and how you would handle a sudden squeezing of a thirty-minute presentation into ten minutes. If you've prepared pictorial visuals, you're fortunate, because your task will be 100 percent easier than the amateur who has all word/number visuals.

To contradict myself—don't be bullied in a competitive presentation. If you sense that your listeners are a little too impatient, don't accept a ten-minute limitation. If your four competitors got thirty minutes, why should you be hamstrung by ten minutes? Tactfully inform your prospect that you're sorry to hear that they are bushed or very busy but that on the spot you can't squeeze thirty minutes into ten. You'd be open, however, to going home, reworking your presentation, redrawing the visuals, pulling team members off the line for more rehearsals, and *then* coming back in two weeks with a dynamite shortened presentation!

"After all," you tell the prospect, "I know how important our presentation is to your company and *ours!*" If they're bushed and bored, a rescheduling would certainly be to your advantage.

▶Client Seminars

Successful speakers at client seminars walk a fine line between advice and entertainment. Many accounting, law, and consulting firms forget this every year when they hold seminars for their clients. A parade of knowledgeable but dull presenters strolls to the lectern and reads the latest tax rulings, estate-planning schemes, or marketing strategies. Service firms think the entertainment part of a presentation means holding these seminars at a pretentious hotel and giving out whiskey and hors d'oeuvres after the presentation.

What a waste. Of course, the listeners think it's o.k.—an afternoon away from the office, free liquor, and good food. But the drawing card is rarely the presenters, nor will the information stick for very long.

Because client seminars walk this fine line between advice and entertainment, pictorial visuals are a must for home-run presentations. If speakers read their presentations, stand behind the lectern, or use word/number visuals, they won't even get to first base.

▶**Multimedia Shows**

I see too many con jobs at large national meetings. The sting is the multimedia extravaganza—four screens and multiple projectors. What is seen is a show, a substitute for the real thing —the presenter.

If you're a weak-kneed vice president who has the charisma of a fruit fly, by all means turn down the lights, lower four screens, and be dwarfed by a multimedia presentation. If you're selling yourself and your ideas, stick with one screen and pictorial visuals.

Some communications firms argue that multimedia presentations are a necessity. They rationalize that salespeople are poor presenters. "We've got to do something to help them!" Some may be poor presenters, but the answer is not to give presenters crutches so they can hobble faster. If credibility, quality, reputation, and service are part of the message, companies should train their people to present instead of letting them narrate in the dark.

Wrong Multimedia Presentation

▶ Courtroom Presentations

If you appear as an expert witness, here's how to strengthen your case: Jam all your content into a persuasive but brief presentation, take the burrs off your delivery, and show only pictorial visuals.

A Persuasive Message

The successful expert witnesses and litigation-support people I've worked with have a knack for condensing a lot of ideas into a brief, persuasive message. They come quickly to the heart of their arguments. They take to card organizing, Chapter 3, like an eight-year-old to candy.

A Controlled Delivery

Nervousness cuts a ragged edge on an expert witness's credibility. Good delivery skills, especially eye contact and a strong voice, are vital if you expect the jury to buy your act without doubts.

Pictorial Visuals

Jurors need, in the worst way, to understand an expert witness's overall concepts, not the nitty-gritty. Jurors often get lost and bored in the detailed word/number visuals—so they may doze. Pictorial visuals are a must, especially for longer trials, when you're counting on the jurors' recall or understanding of technical evidence.

Overloaded Jury

►8◄

Selecting
a Communications Consultant

To profit from good advise requires more wisdom than to give it.—Churton Collins

---

If you're planning to hire a consultant to help you deliver an important presentation, proceed with caution. Unfortunately, there are too many inexperienced trainers in this business. Many hacks teach seminars and try to sell the Brooklyn Bridge. Not only has a cottage industry sprung up, but there are now a handful of firms, with multiple offices, claiming to be experts in platform skills. A large number of these "experts" are poorly trained and understand little about what they are teaching.

Ask for the résumé of the instructor who will work with you. Where did all this vast knowledge he or she is peddling come from? What was he or she before jumping into the communications business? If he or she left the armed service, taught skiing for a while, became a data analyst, fooled around in the advertising world, and then hung ten as a communications consultant, I advise you to go elsewhere.

When consultants appear at your office, ask them the last five books they've read in the communications field and what ideas they agreed or disagreed with. Good communications consultants should be prolific readers. If they're not recharging their own batteries, their information could be dated and shallow.

Be wary of university professors as communications consultants. The credit for the technical advancements of our country is due, in good part, to our excellent schooling. However, two areas in which schools have burdened us with wrong advice are writing and speaking.

Schooling is responsible for the false idea that, in writing, "bulk equals importance." Remember the three-thousand-word essay? Adults who learned as students to pad assignments to gain required length will easily accept the notion that a hundred-page business proposal is more impressive than fifty pages saying the same thing. Whoever got an A for conciseness? That is why accountants, lawyers, and consultants encase their ideas in so many long sentences and heavy words. Consequently, what they write is not very persuasive.

School speech courses get wrapped up in elocution and voice exercises—mostly worthless. I've yet to hear or read about a speech teacher who teaches eye contact. Yet eye contact is one of the most important delivery skills.

The misinformation speech teachers put out is amazing. "Focus on a spot on the back wall, so you won't see all those faces and get nervous," or "To help you feel equal to your audience, look out and imagine them all naked." My God, I have enough trouble in a presentation keeping the content rolling without having to imagine how a mixed audience looks minus its clothes! (Write me some of the dumb advice you've been told and I'll include it in the next printing.)

Motivational Speakers

If you're thinking of hiring a motivational speaker to help you with an important presentation, you're making a mistake. Motivational speakers are usually well-known athletes or salespeople who now make their living speaking at sales meetings or national gatherings.

What these speakers do they do extremely well. That is,

motivate an audience very quickly. One ingredient makes their success possible—enthusiasm!

We all need to be spiritually uplifted. That's why millions attend church. Our business batteries also need recharging. Having Olympic champions, football stars, or super-salespeople tell about their struggle to be the best can be an excellent way to convince listeners that, if they struggle harder, they too will be rewarded. It's an excellent message and a good way to boost morale.

But what about delivery skills? Motivational speakers make the same mistakes business executives do. They pace back and forth, clutching a microphone, and use little eye contact. But all their sins are masked because they have one thing driving them—enthusiasm. Their volume is twice what any business executive would dare voice. Even when he holds a mike, a motivational speaker conveys ten times more action in his free arm than most executives have with two.

Being physical is what athletics is all about. So it should be obvious that it's an easy transition for a football or Olympic star to grunt, groan, shout, and pound on the lectern to make his point. The audience expects it and claps. But a show of physical strength and confidence doesn't make a motivational speaker a delivery-skills teacher.

►9◄

Getting Started

There's a geometric progression in ability: you need to be only 10 percent better at what you do than most people in order to go 100 percent farther.—Sydney J. Harris

---

There's a direct relationship between one's ability to sell ideas to a group and one's advancement.

What better opportunity than a presentation to boost your career? It's on your terms; you control what's said, how it's said, and what's shown. It's a performance in front of some of the most important people in the world—those who judge you, those who buy from you.

Now that you've read the book, it's time to stand and be more persuasive. But perhaps you're thinking, "Will eye contact, pauses, and louder volume really work? Do I dare show pictorial visuals?" Well, I know a terrific way to find out.

Toastmasters International Clubs. They offer an invaluable opportunity—the chance to practice speaking in front of a group at no risk. Toastmasters are strangers in the same lifeboat; there is no danger that they'll hold it against you, or your career, if your delivery stumbles.

Toastmasters is perfect for trying all those physical skills: extended eye contact, hands out of the pockets, a correct stance, bold gestures, strong volume, and long pauses.

Unfortunately, there is no substitute for scrimmaging.

Toastmasters offers the best practice field I know with no chance of career injuries.

> *There is no other accomplishment which any person can have which will so quickly make a career and secure recognition as the ability to speak.*—Phillip D. Armour

Recommended Reading

▶**Musts for the Professional**

Classen, George, *Better Business English,* ARCO Publishing
    Co., 1966.
Fisher, Roger, and William Ury, *Getting to Yes,* Penguin
    Books, 1981.
Jay, Anthony, *The New Oratory,* AMA, Inc., 1971.
Lakein, Alan, *How to Control Your Time,* New American Li-
    brary, 1973.
Meuse, Leonard F., Jr., *Mastering the Business and Technical
    Presentation,* CBI Publishing Co., 1980.
Molloy, John, *Dress for Success,* Warner Books, 1976.
———, *The Woman's Dress for Success,* Follett, 1977.
Ogilvy, David, *Ogilvy on Advertising,* Crown Publishers, 1983.
Simmons, S. H., *How to Be the Life of the Podium,* AMACOM,
    1982.
Sommet, Robert, *The Mind's Eye,* Dell, 1978.
Van Oech, Roger, *A Whack on the Side of the Head,* Warner
    Communications, 1983.

For the Second Round

Carnegie, Dale, *Effective Speaking,* Pocket Books, 1977.

Gunning, Robert, *The Technique of Clear Writing,* revised edition, McGraw-Hill, 1968.

Hodnett, Edward, *Effective Presentations,* Parker Publishing Co., 1967.

Mander, Jerry, *Four Arguments for the Elimination of TV,* William Morrow, 1977.

Nightingale, Earl, *This Is Earl Nightingale,* Nightingale-Conant Corp., 1977.

Quick, John, *A Short Book on the Subject of Public Speaking,* McGraw-Hill, 1978.

Ries, Al, and Jack Trout, *Positioning: The Battle for Your Mind,* McGraw-Hill, 1981.

Samuels, Mike and Nancy Samuels, *Seeing with the Mind's Eye,* Random House, 1975.

Ringer, Robert J., *Restoring the American Dream,* Fawcett, 1980.

Thourlby, William, *You Are What You Wear,* Sheed Andrews and McMeel, 1978.

Townsend, Robert, *Further Up the Organization,* Knopf, 1984.

Good Luck

Call or write for "Persuasive Presentations" or "Effective Writing"
seminars, live and on videotape, and consulting help:
Twain Associates
P. O. Box 449
Wheaton, Illinois 60189
312/665-9370

Index